Don't Panic—
Quick, Easy, *and*
DELICIOUS MEALS
for Your Family

Other books by
Susie Martinez, Vanda Howell,
and Bonnie Garcia

Don't Panic—Dinner's in the Freezer

Don't Panic—More Dinner's in the Freezer

Don't Panic— Quick, Easy, *and* DELICIOUS MEALS *for* Your Family

Susie Martinez
Vanda Howell
and Bonnie Garcia

Revell

a division of Baker Publishing Group
Grand Rapids, Michigan

Published by Revell
a division of Baker Publishing Group
P.O. Box 6287, Grand Rapids, MI 49516-6287
www.revellbooks.com

Printed in the United States of America

Library of Congress Cataloging-in-Publication Data
Martinez, Susie.
    Don't panic—quick, easy, and delicious meals for your family / Susie Martinez,
Vanda Howell, and Bonnie Garcia.
        p.   cm.
    Includes index.
    ISBN 978-0-8007-1994-4 (pbk.)
    1. Quick and easy cooking. 2. Cookbooks. I. Howell, Vanda, II. Garcia, Bonnie.
III. Title.
TX833.5.M37 2012
641.5′55—dc23   2011039109

The internet addresses, email addresses, and phone numbers in this book are accurate at
the time of publication. They are provided as a resource. Baker Publishing Group does
not endorse them or vouch for their content or permanence.

12   13   14   15   16   17   18   7   6   5   4   3   2   1

Susie's Dedication

Susie Martinez dedicates this book in loving memory of Laurel McGilchrist, a beautiful and trusted friend. I am so thankful you shared your life with me, Laurel. As we navigated our way through life's joys and heartaches over the years, you were there to listen, care, and love magnificently. In your exhausting battle with a disease that would steal like a thief, you exhibited unfailing faith and trust in God. I saw him walk with you, hold you, and bring you peace. I watched in complete awe as you touched the lives of many for his glory. Although time with you was too short, I know that you are now with God, free from pain and suffering. You were a gracious and delightful light in my life. I love you, my friend, and even as you live forever in my heart, I miss you always.

Vanda's Dedication

Vanda Howell dedicates this book to: my husband, Mike, who is always so grateful for whatever meal I put before him (whether at 6 p.m. or 9 p.m.). To my son, Elliott, who appointed himself as my personal "food critic": with your love for food (and superfast metabolism) I have no doubt that one day you will become a professional food critic. To my mom, brother, sister, and their families—Flo Kitashima; Tim, Shirlene, and Ani Kulin (*Ani, we waited so long to finally have you here—you are amazing!*); and Bryan, Shari, and Lucca Kitashima (*Lucca, even though we are an ocean apart, I get to see you grow up via your dad's proud [constant] videos/pics and emails.*): thanks to all of you for always being my encouragement—I love you all very much!

Bonnie's Dedication

Bonnie would like to dedicate this latest Don't Panic project to her family: you have been with me through every step of the journey. From the time the first Don't Panic book came into being over fourteen years ago to now, you have believed in me and cheered me on. Even when I thought the last book had been written, you encouraged me to keep cooking and keep writing. Steve, Nathan, Daniel, and Johnny—I love you with all my heart.

Contents

Preface

We all need to eat. And someone is generally assigned the job of making sure we eat. Whoever has this duty eventually becomes exhausted with the endless task and begins to seek assistance.

The previous two Don't Panic cookbooks helped you store dinners in your freezer so they were on hand in a moment's notice. This book also follows the concept of readily available meals but approaches the mission in another way. Here we provide you with recipes that require 30 minutes or less of "hands-on" preparation time. And the meals are fantastic.

We are so excited about every recipe selection you will find here! When this book was complete, our families went through mourning because the anticipation of what new and spectacular savory delight would appear on our tables each week had come to an end. But for you, the journey is about to begin.

So gather your loved ones around the table tonight and serve them something quick, delicious, and brand-new for dinner. Your taste buds will think they have gone somewhere wonderful for vacation. Enjoy!

Acknowledgments

Thank you to so many of our dear friends and readers for your input, comments, and support over the years. To those of you who contributed to this book through proofreading, taste testing, and recipe submissions, we thank you. We would like to acknowledge the following people whose recipes were included in this book. In our opinion these recipes are real "winners"!

Laura Beutler
Shirley Burke
Alivia Butler
Shannon Butler
Virginia Cebell
Lori Fox
Beverly Garrison
Cathy Healy
Jodi Heiser
Ruth Holm
Tylene Howell

Susan Jones
Cassie Martinez
Donna Mayberry
Heidi Messer
AnnMarie Moseley
Paula Rome
Jack Sunahara
Marcia Sunahara
Debbie White
Jeanie Wilking
Pam Zundel

Introduction

Simple and Easy . . . at Last!

Many things in life are simple in concept yet not very easy to do. We run into these things every day. For many of us, cooking at home is like this. It is simple in concept, but it isn't easy to pull off. In fact, the task of riffling through recipes and preparing a meal has been known to drive many women out the front door and straight to a "chick-flick" at the end of the day . . . leaving behind her husband, kids, and dog to fend for themselves.

If you are familiar with the previous Don't Panic cookbooks, then you know we base our books on a few simple concepts.

First, we provide you with recipes that truly taste good. Most cookbooks contain a greater volume of recipes than you'll find in the Don't Panic cookbooks. However, in those books you have to kiss a lot of frogs before you meet your prince. You may find one or two recipes in a book that you like and your family will eat. Then you put the book away until you make that meal again. Every recipe in our books tastes great because we work with a recipe until it meets our highly selective standards. So you can rest assured that you will enjoy the meal you put your time, energy, and money into preparing.

(One *really* fun thing in writing this book is we are finally able to share some of our longtime favorite recipes with you that we left out of our previous books because they are not suitable for the freezer.)

Second, the ingredients are items you can pronounce and are usually found in your kitchen. Our recipes do not require a Google search to define or a scavenger hunt to the next town to locate the ingredients.

Third, we help you simplify meal preparation and get the most out of the amount of time and energy you invest. Our first two Don't Panic books are freezer cookbooks—they teach a simple method of cooking that leaves your freezer full of wonderful meals.

This book takes a different turn and helps you conserve time and energy by providing you with delicious recipes that can be prepared in a short amount of time. So, with this book, we offer you one thing that is truly simple *and* easy (at last!). If you have 30 minutes (or less) to devote to preparing a meal, then try one of the recipes on the pages that follow. Look forward to the adventure . . . your family, friends, and guests will think that you cooked all day!

Susie

Cooking Quick and Easy

Let's face it; most of us live life on the run. And the three of us can attest we are no exception! As has always been the case, we are forever on a quest for how to make life easier, especially in the kitchen. Hopefully the recipes in this book will help you get dinner on the table quickly—with less than 30 minutes of hands-on prep time. We have a few other suggestions from personal experience that you might find helpful as well:

Plan out five meals for the week and incorporate them into a weekly meal calendar. The other two nights of the week, eat leftovers or treat yourself to takeout!

Invest in a warehouse membership and use it to buy large pantry items such as foil, plastic wrap, and freezer bags. Also, other staples such as cheese, butter, eggs, soy sauce, nuts, chocolate chips, vanilla, olive oil, spices, and seasonings are much more reasonably priced than at the local grocery store. If you don't have a large family, consider going in with a friend and splitting up the goods! However, we have found the best bet for meat prices is the weekly loss leaders at your local grocery store (see next suggestion).

Shop the loss leaders. Local grocery stores feature "loss leader" items each week that they advertise in their weekly ads. Get in the habit of checking these out each week and cooking according to what's on sale. You will save a ton just by doing this one simple step. For example, when chicken is on sale, try to feature chicken recipes at least a couple of times during that week. Also, prepare at least one chicken recipe that can be frozen and make it in quantity—have one for dinner and freeze the remainder to be used down the road when life is especially hectic.

Organize your trips to the grocery store. You will save time and money by planning out your meals. It will keep you from spending money on "impulse buys," and you will save time by going to the grocery store less often. I find I am much more organized and efficient if I have my planned weekly menu in front of me and construct my shopping list based on the menu before I ever walk into the store! Consider making a "blueprint" of your grocery store and listing the items on your shopping list according to your grocery store layout.

Keep regular inventory items on hand. As you get started, keep track of the recipes you use over the course of a month. Look at common ingredients you use over and over again, and get in the habit of keeping these items on hand. This will keep you from making unneeded trips to the grocery store for one or two items and will save you time and money! Common ingredients we use in this book include the following.

Pantry Items

Baking ingredients: flour, sugar, brown sugar, powdered sugar, baking soda, baking powder, vanilla, chocolate chips

Canned goods: tomato products, diced green chiles, broths, jalapeño peppers, black beans, refried beans

Condiments: vinegars, pickles, mustards, ketchup, olives, sun-dried tomatoes, pesto, salsa

Dried herbs and spices: kosher salt, pepper (fine and course), red pepper flakes, cayenne pepper, ginger, garlic salt, chili powder, cinnamon

Long grain rice

Noodles and pastas: ziti, penne, fettuccine, spaghetti

Nuts: almonds, walnuts, pecans, cashews

Oils: olive, canola, sesame, peanut

Onion soup mix

Peanut butter, honey, maple syrup

Steak sauce, hot pepper sauce, hoisin sauce, soy sauce, chili sauce

Perishables

Cheeses: cheddar, Monterey jack, mozzarella, cream cheese, parmesan

Dairy: milk, yogurt, sour cream, butter, eggs, mayonnaise

Ingredients for fresh salad

Lemons, oranges, limes

Onions, garlic, shallots, green onion, fresh ginger

You get the idea!

Deciphering the Code

 = Lighter Fare

These recipes are considered Lighter Fare because they are lower in either Total Calories, Total Fat, or Total Carbohydrates, but not necessarily all of these areas. The nutritional information listed on each recipe is approximate. If more precise calculations are needed, please consult a dietician.

 = Quick

These recipes are considered quick because the total time to make this meal is 30 minutes or less from beginning to end.

 = Entertaining

These are recipes that we personally serve to dinner guests.

 = 6 Ingredients or Less

These are recipes that use 6 ingredients or less (excluding salt, pepper, or water).

 **= Authors' Top Three Picks**

These are our favorite recipes; there are three per section, one for each of us.

= Meals That Can Be Frozen

These are recipes that can be frozen. They include a quantity table for the recipe, just like our previous two cookbooks. This allows you to make several of this entrée at once and freeze the extras. We suggest you use our freezer bag method of freezing for recipes containing this icon.

Freezer Bag Method

- *When to use it*:

    Liquid: Use this method when freezing items such as soup, chili, and stew.

    Semisolid Food Items: Use this method when freezing items that DO NOT need to hold a particular form, such as meats in marinade, stroganoff, and barbecue shredded beef.

- *How to do it*: When using the freezer bag method, place your meal in the freezer bag, remove as much air as possible, and seal. Then take a cake pan, or another pan with sides, and lay the bags flat, stacking one on top of the other in the pan. The cake pan will not only freeze the meals flat, giving you more freezer room, but will also help ensure that any leaks will be kept within the pan. Place the pan in the freezer. Once the items have been flash frozen, remove them from the pan and stack the bags inside your freezer. Meals that are frozen flat thaw much more quickly than meals put in the freezer in a random clump.

- *On serving day*: When defrosting, make sure you place the item in the refrigerator with a pan, plate, or bowl underneath to catch the extra moisture (or leaks) from defrosting. For your health and safe food handling, we do not recommend defrosting the meal on the kitchen countertop, as this promotes the growth of harmful bacteria. If you need to speed up the defrosting process, consider using the defrost cycle on your microwave oven.

For more freezer-friendly recipes and in-depth information on how to successfully freeze meals, check out our previous books: *Don't Panic—Dinner's in the Freezer* and *Don't Panic—More Dinner's in the Freezer*.

Small Bites and Appetizers

Blackened Chicken Quesadillas
Burger Bites
Eggplant and White Bean Italian
    Hummus
Farmer's Cheese Flatbread
Ginger Cream Cheese Ball
Luscious Lamb Meatballs with
    Cilantro Dipping Sauce
Mashed Potatoes in Golden Phyllo
    Dough
Mini Turkey Focaccia Sandwiches
Rich and Creamy Cheese Fondue
Roasted Garlic Crostini
Sausage Bites
Savory Baked Potato Bites
Southwestern Baked Cheese Dip
Spicy Pecans
Super Salsa

Blackened Chicken Quesadillas

A favorite family treat with a Cajun kick!

4 boneless, skinless chicken breasts

2 T. Cajun spice blend

8 flour tortillas

4 cups fontina cheese, shredded, divided

Options for Serving

salsa

sour cream

guacamole

Recipe Yield	**Prep Time**	**Total Time**
8 servings	20 minutes	25 minutes

Directions

Coat chicken breasts with Cajun spice (store purchased, or use the Cajun seasoning recipe for Cajun Mahi Mahi on page 164). Sauté chicken in skillet over medium heat until blackened, 4–5 minutes per side. Remove from pan, allow chicken to rest 5 minutes, then slice across the grain approx. ½-inch thick.

Coat a nonstick pan with cooking spray and heat over medium heat. Place a tortilla in pan and sprinkle one half of the tortilla with ¼ cup cheese, sliced chicken (about half a breast), and another ¼ cup cheese. Fold empty side over and cook until golden on each side. Slice into wedges. Repeat with remaining tortillas. Serve warm with salsa, sour cream, and/or guacamole.

Nutritional Information (per quesadilla): Calories 489.6; Total Fat 24.0g; Cholesterol 72.9mg; Sodium 640.2mg; Total Carbohydrates 41.8g (Dietary Fiber 0.0g); Protein 24.9g

Burger Bites

A delicious addition to any football gathering.

2 eggs
½ t. salt
¼ t. pepper
1½ t. Worcestershire sauce
2 T. ketchup
2 cloves garlic, minced or pressed
1–2 T. parsley
½ t. red pepper flakes or cayenne pepper (optional)
1½ lbs. ground beef, bison, turkey, or chicken
½ cup panko breadcrumbs* (or regular breadcrumbs)
¼ cup parmesan cheese
cocktail rolls or dinner rolls (such as Sweet Hawaiian) for serving

Suggested Toppers

barbecue sauce
cheese slices
grilled onions (slice 3 whole onions, cook over medium heat in 2 T. olive oil and ½ t. salt until tender and carmelized)
crisp bacon slices

*Panko breadcrumbs can be found in the Asian/ethnic aisles of most grocery stores or in larger quantities in Asian markets. Panko crumbs are much lighter than regular breadcrumbs, and make a crunchier coating when baked or fried.

Recipe Yield	**Prep Time**	**Total Time**
4–6 servings (8–12 mini-burgers)	15 minutes	30 minutes

Directions

In a medium mixing bowl, beat eggs with salt, pepper, Worcestershire sauce, ketchup, garlic, parsley, and red pepper flakes until blended. Place meat on top of egg mixture, then pour the panko crumbs and parmesan cheese on top of meat. Using your hands, mix everything together just until all ingredients are incorporated (see tip). Do not overmix.

Form mini-patties that are approximately 2 inches in diameter and ½-inch thick, and place on platter. Spray tops lightly with cooking spray.

Preheat gas grill to medium (or heat a griddle or frying pan over medium heat). Grill or panfry patties for 8–10 minutes to desired doneness, turning once during cooking time.

Place mini-burgers on rolls and set out toppers for everyone to customize their burgers.

Nutritional Information (per serving): Calories 437.2; Total Fat 33.6g; Cholesterol 167.2mg; Sodium 405.4mg; Total Carbohydrates 8.8g (Dietary Fiber 0.5g); Protein 23.5g

Tip

For a quick cleanup and no messy hands, wear disposable latex gloves when you mix with your hands.

Eggplant and White Bean Italian Hummus

The combination of roasted eggplant and beans gives this hummus dip a rich, buttery taste.

1–1½ lb. eggplant or Japanese eggplant, peeled and cut into 1½–2 inch pieces*
½ cup olive oil, divided
1–15 oz. can white cannellini beans (or white kidney beans), drained and rinsed
⅓ cup Italian parsley
3 T. fresh lemon juice (approx. 1 medium lemon)
½ t. salt
¼ t. pepper
1 garlic clove
¼ t. cayenne pepper or red pepper flakes
parchment paper (optional)
pita chips or assorted crackers for dipping

*Japanese eggplants are smaller and thinner. Use 3–5, or enough to equal 1½ lbs.

Recipe Yield	**Prep Time**	**Total Time**
6 servings	30 minutes	30–45 minutes

Directions

Preheat oven to 450 degrees, placing oven rack in middle position. Line a baking sheet with parchment paper or spray sheet with cooking spray; place the cut-up eggplant on baking sheet in a single layer. Drizzle eggplant with 3–4 T. of olive oil, followed by a sprinkling of salt and pepper. Roast eggplant for 20 to 25 minutes or until golden brown. Cool.

While the eggplant is roasting, place beans, parsley, lemon juice, ½ t. salt, ¼ t. pepper, garlic, and cayenne pepper into a food processor bowl or blender. Pulse a few times until mixture is coarsely chopped. Add cooked eggplant to mixture and pulse a few more times.

Turn the food processor on and gradually add ¼ cup of olive oil, or more if needed, until the mixture comes to a creamy consistency. Add more salt, pepper, or cayenne pepper to taste. Place hummus dip in a serving bowl. Serve with pita chips or crackers.

Nutritional Information (per serving): Calories 259.3; Total Fat 18.5g; Cholesterol 0.0mg; Sodium 489.6mg; Total Carbohydrates 19.9g (Dietary Fiber 7.9g); Protein 5.6g

Farmer's Cheese Flatbread

Simple yet deceivingly good—be sure to make extra!

2 rounds pita bread, unsplit
1 cup farmer's or Monterey jack cheese, shredded
½ t. dried oregano
½ t. salt
¼ t. pepper

Recipe Yield	Prep Time	Total Time
8 servings	5 minutes	10 minutes

Directions

Line a jelly roll pan with foil. Preheat broiler. Place both pitas on foil-lined pan. Sprinkle each pita with cheese, then oregano, salt, and pepper, dividing quantities evenly between each pita. Place under broiler in oven. Broil for 3–5 minutes until golden brown and cheese is bubbly. Cut into wedges and serve immediately. Wonderful served alone or with warm marinara sauce!

Nutritional Information (per serving): Calories 122.0; Total Fat 5.2g; Cholesterol 20.0mg; Sodium 465.8mg; Total Carbohydrates 8.5g (Dietary Fiber 0.4g); Protein 9.4g

Ginger Cream Cheese Ball

A great holiday appetizer!

Contributed by Susan Jones—Centennial, Colorado

8 oz. pitted dates
8 candied ginger bits*
½ cup pecans
2–8 oz. pkgs. cream cheese, softened
½ cup flaked coconut
gingersnaps, for serving

*Candied ginger bits can be found in the spices/seasoning section of the grocery store.

Recipe Yield

12 servings

Prep Time

10 minutes

Total Time

2 hours 10 minutes

Directions

Coarsely chop dates, candied ginger, and pecans in food processor. Add cream cheese and blend until smooth. Chill for 2 hours in refrigerator, then shape into 1 large cheese ball or 2 smaller balls. Roll cheese ball in flaked coconut to cover. Serve with gingersnaps such as Pepperidge Farm mini-gingerbread cookies.

Nutritional Information (per serving): Calories 224.0; Total Fat 17.9g; Cholesterol 41.6mg; Sodium 113.3mg; Total Carbohydrates 14.4g (Dietary Fiber 2.0g); Protein 3.8g

Luscious Lamb Meatballs with Cilantro Dipping Sauce

Just when you thought you didn't like lamb.

2 T. olive oil
1 small onion, finely diced
1 lb. ground lamb
2 eggs, lightly beaten
½ cup fresh parsley
2 T. breadcrumbs
1 t. ground cumin
3 cloves garlic, minced
1 t. salt
½ t. pepper

Dipping Sauce

1 cup plain yogurt (Greek style preferred)
2 T. fresh cilantro, chopped
1 clove garlic, minced
¼ t. salt

Recipe Yield	**Prep Time**	**Total Time**
42 meatballs	20–25 minutes	35–45 minutes

Directions

Preheat oven to 400 degrees. Lightly oil a rimmed baking sheet. Heat olive oil in a medium skillet over medium heat. Add onions and sauté until soft, about 5 minutes. Transfer the onions to a large mixing bowl and add remaining ingredients. Using your hands, combine the ingredients just until mixed—don't overwork the meat mixture. Form the lamb mixture into 1-inch balls, rolling them lightly between your palms. Place on the prepared baking sheet. Bake meatballs, turning once, until evenly browned, about 8–12 minutes. While meatballs are baking, prepare the dipping sauce.

For dipping sauce: in a small bowl whisk together the yogurt, cilantro, garlic, and salt. Chill slightly.

Arrange cooked meatballs on a serving platter. Secure each meatball with a toothpick and serve with dipping sauce.

Nutritional Information (per 2 meatballs): Calories 74.3; Total Fat 6.0g; Cholesterol 31.5mg; Sodium 114.3mg; Total Carbohydrates 0.6g (Dietary Fiber 0.1g); Protein 3.8g

Tip

For a quick cleanup and no messy hands, wear disposable latex gloves when you mix with your hands.

Mashed Potatoes in Golden Phyllo Dough

A unique and surprising appetizer your guests will love!

3 cups mashed potatoes (instant potatoes work fine)
1½ t. salt
8 sheets phyllo dough
¼ cup butter, melted
1 cup cheddar cheese, shredded and divided
3 strips bacon, fried crisp and crumbled

Options for Serving

sour cream
green onions

Recipe Yield	**Prep Time**	**Total Time**
12 servings	30 minutes	40 minutes

Directions

Preheat oven to 350 degrees. Prepare mashed potatoes (if using instant potatoes, prepare according to package directions); add salt and stir. Place potatoes in a gallon-sized freezer or storage bag and make a small diagonal cut across bottom corner of bag. Set aside.

Open and unfold phyllo dough. Lay a damp towel over the dough unless working with it; this will keep it moist enough to roll without tearing. Brush one side of a sheet of phyllo dough with melted butter and then place a second sheet over it. Butter the top of the second sheet of dough. Pipe an inch-thick "line" of mashed potatoes down the long side of the prepared phyllo dough sheets (approximately 1 inch in from the edge of the dough). Fold the edge of the phyllo dough sheets over the mashed potatoes and continue to roll the mashed potatoes in the dough jelly roll style, creating a log. Brush with butter. Repeat this process 3 additional times to form a total of 4 logs.

Place logs on a greased cookie sheet and bake until golden brown (approximately 8–10 minutes). When phyllo dough is just beginning to turn golden, sprinkle shredded cheese on top of each log and continue to bake until cheese is melted. Remove from oven and sprinkle with crumbled bacon. Cut each log into 2-inch segments and serve.

If desired, sprinkle with green onion slices and provide sour cream for dipping.

Nutritional Information (per serving): Calories 168.5; Total Fat 9.6g; Cholesterol 25.0mg; Sodium 624.0mg; Total Carbohydrates 16.0g (Dietary Fiber 1.3g); Protein 5.2g

Mini Turkey Focaccia Sandwiches

The basil and herb filling makes this worth the effort!

Contributed by Tylene Howell—Golden, Colorado

Focaccia

| 1–13.8 oz. pkg. refrigerated pizza crust (such as Pillsbury) |
| 1 T. olive or canola oil |
| ½ T. garlic powder |
| ½ t. dry Italian seasoning |
| ½ cup shredded parmesan cheese |

Filling

| 1–6.5 oz. container herb and garlic cream cheese, softened |
| 2 medium Roma tomatoes, thinly sliced |
| 1 bunch fresh basil leaves, stems removed |
| ½ lb. smoked deli turkey, thinly sliced |
| 30–40 toothpicks |

Recipe Yield	**Prep Time**	**Total Time**
35–40 mini-sandwiches	35 minutes	45–50 minutes

Directions

Heat oven to 400 degrees. Spray a large cookie sheet with cooking spray. Unroll pizza crust dough and press onto cookie sheet. Using your fingers or the end of a wooden spoon, press shallow indentations into dough approximately every inch. Brush pizza dough with olive oil. Mix garlic powder, Italian seasoning, and parmesan cheese in a small bowl. Sprinkle evenly onto dough. Bake for 10–13 minutes or until golden brown. Let cool for 15–20 minutes then cut in half horizontally like a sandwich roll.

Turn over one of the halves of the focaccia and spread the bottom with cream cheese. Working across the bread, top with a single layer of tomatoes and then basil, spacing toppings out every 1½ inches. Next, layer turkey evenly over basil. Place the top of the focaccia cut side down over turkey; press down. With toothpicks, pierce through all layers so sandwiches will hold together. Cut between toothpicks with a long, serrated knife to make 35–40 sandwich squares.

Nutritional Information (per mini-sandwich): Calories 51.1; Total Fat 3.0g; Cholesterol 7.5mg; Sodium 139.2mg; Total Carbohydrates 1.6g (Dietary Fiber 0.1g); Protein 2.4g

Rich and Creamy Cheese Fondue

Entertaining and appetizing . . . your guests will love it!

| 1 garlic clove, halved crosswise |
| 1½ cups dry white wine |
| ½ lb. Emmental cheese, coarsely grated (2 cups) |
| ½ lb. Gruyère, coarsely grated (2 cups) |
| 2 T. cornstarch |

For Dipping

| bread cubes (French, sourdough, rye, etc.) |
| apples, sliced and cored |

Recipe Yield

8 servings

Prep Time

25 minutes

Total Time

25 minutes

Directions

Rub inside of a heavy 4-quart pot with cut sides of garlic, then discard garlic. Add wine to pot and bring just to a simmer over moderate heat.

Place grated cheeses in a large mixing bowl and sprinkle cornstarch on top. Gently toss cheese to coat with cornstarch.

Gradually add cheese to simmering wine and cook, stirring constantly in a zigzag pattern (not a circular motion) to prevent cheese from balling up, until cheese is just melted (it will get a bit stringy first) and creamy. Do not boil. Bring fondue to a gentle simmer and cook, stirring, until thickened, 5–8 minutes.

Transfer to fondue pot and serve warm with bread and apples for dipping.

Nutritional Information (per serving): Calories 185.0; Total Fat 11.8g; Cholesterol 39.1mg; Sodium 114.3mg; Total Carbohydrates 1.8g (Dietary Fiber 0.0g); Protein 12.1g

Roasted Garlic Crostini

Always a crowd-pleaser!

Roasted Garlic

4 heads garlic

¼ cup olive oil

Crostini

12–½-inch slices of baguette-style Italian bread, sliced at a 45-degree angle

¼ cup extra virgin olive oil

puréed garlic from 4 whole roasted heads of garlic (see above)

Topping Options

shaved parmesan or Gruyère cheese

fresh, creamy goat cheese, at room temperature

roasted red peppers, home-roasted or bottled, cut into thin strips

oil-packed sun-dried tomatoes, cut into thin strips

fresh mozzarella cheese, sliced

capers, drained

Roma tomatoes, thinly sliced, or halved, seeded, and diced

fresh basil leaves, cut into fine julienne strips or left whole

crushed red pepper flakes

balsamic vinegar

thinly sliced prosciutto

anchovy fillets packed in olive oil, drained

Recipe Yield	Prep Time	Total Time
4 servings	25 minutes	90 minutes

Directions

To roast garlic, preheat oven to 375 degrees. Place garlic in a small roasting pan and drizzle with olive oil. Toss to coat thoroughly. Bake for 50–60 minutes or until garlic bulbs are very tender but not overly brown. Bulbs will be soft when given a gentle squeeze (protect your hand with a folded kitchen towel or oven glove). Remove garlic from the oven and allow to cool.

Using a sharp serrated knife, cut each head of roasted garlic in half crosswise, midway between top and bottom, to expose all the cloves inside. Their pulp will be golden brown and soft. Squeeze the garlic out of each half by hand or scoop it out with a small spoon or knife. Transfer the roasted garlic to a small bowl; pour in any olive oil from the baking dish and mash garlic with a fork to form a smooth purée. You'll have ⅓ to ½ cup of purée, depending on the size of the garlic heads.

To make the Roasted Garlic Crostini, brush bread slices with olive oil and arrange them on a baking sheet. Bake in a 375 degree oven until golden brown, 12–15 minutes. Remove slices from the oven and cool to room temperature. Spread the puréed garlic evenly on the tops of the crostini. Top with any combination of the options listed above, or set out an assortment for everyone to customize their crostini.

Nutritional Information (per serving without topping): Calories 222.0; Total Fat 14.6g; Cholesterol 0.0mg; Sodium 178.0mg; Total Carbohydrates 21.0g (Dietary Fiber 1.0g); Protein 3.8g

Sausage Bites

A no-fuss appetizer for any occasion.

2 T. unsalted butter
3 T. onion, chopped
1 cup ketchup
2 T. molasses
2 T. lemon juice
2 T. sugar
2 T. cider vinegar
1 T. Worcestershire sauce
1 t. dry mustard
½ t. pepper
14 oz. small cooked sausage links, or cooked kielbasa cut into ½ inch pieces

Recipe Yield

8 servings

Prep Time

20 minutes

Total Time

40 minutes

Directions

For sauce: in medium saucepan, melt butter over low heat. Add onion and sauté until tender. Add all remaining ingredients except sausage, and bring to a boil. Reduce heat to simmer and continue boiling for 15 minutes.

Place sausage in a 2-quart baking dish. Add sauce. Cover and bake in 350 degree oven for 15 minutes or until sauce is bubbly and heated through.

Nutritional Information (per serving): Calories 228.0; Total Fat 14.7g; Cholesterol 34.9mg; Sodium 745.8mg; Total Carbohydrates 19.2g (Dietary Fiber 0.1g); Protein 5.5g

Savory Baked Potato Bites

One bite is not enough!

8 baby potatoes (or new red potatoes), ends trimmed, cut in half crosswise
¼ t. salt
1 T. olive oil
½ cup brown sugar
1¼ t. red chili pepper flakes, divided
10 slices bacon
¼ cup sour cream
2 T. cream cheese, softened
½ t. Dijon mustard

Recipe Yield

16 potato bites

Prep Time

25–30 minutes

Total Time

1 hour 15 minutes

Directions

Toss the first 3 ingredients together on a rimmed baking sheet. Bake in a 400 degree oven for 20–25 minutes or until potatoes are tender. Arrange potatoes, cut side down, on a serving plate. Reduce oven temperature to 350 degrees.

In a small bowl, combine brown sugar and 1 t. chili pepper flakes. Coat bacon slices with brown sugar mixture. Arrange bacon on a wire rack set on a foil-lined baking sheet. Bake at 350 degrees for about 25 minutes or until bacon is browned and glazed. Let cool for 5–10 minutes before finely chopping bacon.

Combine sour cream, cream cheese, mustard, remaining chili pepper flakes, and chopped bacon. Spoon onto potatoes and serve.

Nutritional Information (per potato bite): Calories 135.0; Total Fat 9.3g; Cholesterol 8.0mg; Sodium 145.0mg; Total Carbohydrates 22.0g (Dietary Fiber 2.0g); Protein 4.0g

Southwestern Baked Cheese Dip

Bake and serve in a hollowed-out bread loaf.

2 cups mild Cheddar cheese, shredded
8 oz. cream cheese, softened
1½ cups sour cream
½ cup cooked diced ham
¼ cup chopped mild green chiles
2 T. finely chopped jalapeño peppers (optional)
⅓ cup chopped green onions
⅛ t. Worcestershire sauce
1–1 lb. round loaf of crusty bread

Recipe Yield	**Prep Time**	**Total Time**
8–12 servings	20 minutes	1 hour 20 minutes

Directions

In a medium bowl, combine cheddar cheese, cream cheese, sour cream, ham, chiles, jalapeño peppers, green onions, and Worcestershire sauce. Mix to blend well.

Cut a thin slice from top of bread loaf; set aside. Gently remove the soft center of bread. Fill hollowed bread loaf with dip; cover with reserved top slice of loaf. Wrap the filled loaf in foil. Bake at 350 degrees for 1 hour. Serve with crackers or chips.

Nutritional Information (per ½ cup serving): Calories 394.0; Total Fat 25.8g; Cholesterol 71.0mg; Sodium 626.2mg; Total Carbohydrates 25.8g (Dietary Fiber 1.4g); Protein 14.8g

Spicy Pecans

Amazingly addictive!

Contributed by Pam Zundel—Lakewood, Colorado

1 large egg white
2 T. fresh orange juice
4 cups pecan halves
½ cup sugar
1½ t. salt
1½ t. chili powder
½ t. cayenne pepper
pinch black pepper

Recipe Yield

4 cups

Prep Time

15 minutes

Total Time

1 hour 15 minutes

Directions

In a medium bowl, whisk together egg white and orange juice. Add pecans and toss to coat. Add remaining ingredients and toss again. Line a baking sheet with parchment paper or foil. Spread out pecans on baking sheet. Bake for 1 hour at 225 degrees, stirring every 15 minutes. Cool and store in an airtight container. Great on salads or served with cheese and drinks!

Nutritional Information (per ¼ cup serving): Calories 233.5; Total Fat 21.5g; Cholesterol 0.0mg; Sodium 224.0mg; Total Carbohydrates 11.0g (Dietary Fiber 3.0g); Protein 3.1g

Super Salsa

Serve on the patio at your next summer get together!
Contributed by Donna Mayberry—Denver, Colorado

6 tomatoes, quartered
½ onion, quartered
1 jalapeño pepper, seeded
½ bunch cilantro
1 t. garlic powder
1 t. salt
juice of 1 lime (about 2 T.)
1 cup frozen sweet corn, partially thawed
2 avocados, peeled and cubed

Recipe Yield

10–12 servings

Prep Time

10 minutes

Total Time

10 minutes

Directions

Blend first seven ingredients together in a food processor until coarsely chopped. Spoon into a medium serving bowl. Add sweet corn and avocado; stir salsa ingredients to combine. Serve immediately with chips!

Nutritional Information (per serving): Calories 65; Total Fat 4.7g; Cholesterol 0mg; Sodium 202mg; Total Carbohydrates 6.2g (Dietary Fiber 2.8g); Protein 1.2g

Breakfast, Breads, and Brunch

Barbecue Chicken Wraps

*Great served either warm or cold;
take one to work for lunch tomorrow!*

Chicken

2–3 cups shredded cooked chicken (may use rotisserie chicken)

1 cup barbecue sauce

Filling Ingredients

1½ cups cheddar cheese, shredded

½ head lettuce, shredded

1 tomato, thinly sliced

1 cup tortilla strips

6–12-inch tortilla wraps

ranch or bleu cheese dressing, if desired

Recipe Yield	**Prep Time**	**Total Time**
6 servings	25 minutes	25 minutes

Directions

In medium bowl, mix shredded chicken with barbecue sauce of your choice. Set aside.

Layer ingredients down the center of each tortilla in the following order: cheddar cheese, lettuce, tomato, tortilla strips, and chicken. Drizzle with ranch or bleu cheese dressing (if desired) and roll wrap, tucking in open ends. Slice in half at an angle and serve with fresh fruit.

Nutritional Information (per serving): Calories 401.0; Total Fat 22.7g; Cholesterol 44.4mg; Sodium 820.4mg; Total Carbohydrates 35.0g (Dietary Fiber 4.0g); Protein 16.1g

Chicken Pitas with Sun-Dried Tomato Vinaigrette

A little taste of Italy to take on a picnic!

2 T. balsamic vinegar
1 T. oil-packed sun-dried tomatoes, chopped
4½ t. sun-dried tomato oil (from jar of sun-dried tomatoes)
¼ t. freshly ground black pepper
1 garlic clove, minced
4 cups shredded cooked chicken (may use rotisserie chicken)
1 cup chopped tomato (about 1 medium)
½ cup (2 oz.) grated Asiago cheese
¼ cup thinly sliced fresh basil
6–6-inch pitas, cut in half
3 cups mixed baby greens

Recipe Yield

12 servings

Prep Time

20 minutes

Total Time

20 minutes

Directions

Combine first five ingredients in a large bowl. Stir in chicken, tomato, cheese, and basil. Place ¼ cup greens in each pita half, then fill with chicken mixture.

Nutritional Information (1 stuffed pita half): Calories 171.0; Total Fat 4.55g; Cholesterol 28.0mg; Sodium 198.5mg; Total Carbohydrates 18.6g (Dietary Fiber 1.2g); Protein 13.2g

Cream Cheese Danish

This recipe is like magic; the flavors come alive overnight!

16 oz. cream cheese, softened
2 T. lemon juice
¾ cup sugar
1 t. vanilla
1 egg, separated
2 large packages crescent rolls
1 t. sugar

Recipe Yield
12 servings

Prep Time
15 minutes

Total Time
45 minutes

Directions

Preheat oven to 350 degrees. In a medium bowl, combine cream cheese, lemon juice, ¾ cup sugar, vanilla, and egg yolk. Mix until fluffy.

Unroll one package of crescent rolls. In 9 x 13 pan, lay rolls flat in pan, pressing edges together, to completely cover bottom of pan. Spread cheese mixture over rolls. Use other package of rolls to form top layer of pastry. Bake for 30 minutes.

Add 1 t. sugar to egg white. When Danish is medium brown, remove from oven and brush with egg white mixture. Return to oven until deep brown. Cool.

Optional icing: put 1 cup powdered sugar in small bowl. Add small amount of milk (2–3 T.) and mix until of drizzling consistency. Drizzle icing over Danish.

Let cool overnight in refrigerator before serving (this is very important). Cut into 3-inch squares.

Variations: Add raisins, cherries, blueberries, or other fruits to filling prior to adding top layer of pastry.

Nutritional Information (per serving): Calories 309.0; Total Fat 19.6g; Cholesterol 44.5mg; Sodium 406.0mg; Total Carbohydrates 28.5g (Dietary Fiber .3g); Protein 5.7g

Delicious Granola

You choose the flavor . . . our favorite is caramel!

Contributed by Debbie White—Littleton, Colorado

20 cups (4 lbs.) regular rolled oats
2½ cups (½ lb.) coconut flakes
2 cups (½ lb.) sunflower seeds
1½ cups (½ lb.) cashew pieces
2 cups (½ lb.) walnut pieces
1¼ cups (½ lb.) almond slivers
1–25.4 fl. oz bottle DaVinci gourmet syrup (flavor of your choice)*

*DaVinci syrup may be found in the coffee flavorings section of the grocery store.

Recipe Yield

28 1-cup servings

Prep Time

15 minutes

Total Time

3–4 hours

Directions

Mix all ingredients in a large mixing bowl and then spread on 2 jelly roll pans or rimmed cookie sheets that have been sprayed with cooking spray. Bake at low heat (200 degrees), stirring every 30 minutes, until the granola is no longer moist. Watch carefully to avoid burning. The goal is for the granola to be dry and crispy, and a bit toasty brown.

Nutritional Information (per 1 cup serving): Calories 207.9; Total Fat 17.0g; Cholesterol 0.0mg; Sodium 13.6mg; Total Carbohydrates 9.5g (Dietary Fiber 3.2g); Protein 5.7g

Fresh Fruit Kabobs

The fruit dressing livens up this recipe!

2 cups green seedless grapes
1 whole pineapple, peeled and cut into chunks
1 qt. (4 cups) fresh strawberries, hulled
12 wooden skewers

Dressing

6 oz. can frozen limeade, thawed
1/3 cup canola oil
1/3 cup honey

Recipe Yield	**Prep Time**	**Total Time**
12 servings	30 minutes	1 hour 20 minutes

Directions

Skewer fresh fruit onto wooden skewers as desired. Pour dressing ingredients into blender and blend well. Place fruit skewers in 9 x 13 glass baking dish. Pour dressing over fruit kabobs, cover, and chill in refrigerator for 1 hour. Serve chilled.

Nutritional Information (per serving): Calories 135.0; Total Fat 6.6g; Cholesterol 0.0mg, Sodium 2.2mg; Total Carbohydrates 23.1g (Dietary Fiber 2.1g); Protein 0.7g

Grilled Garlic Bread

One of Johnny Garcia's favorites!

| 1 loaf French bread (12 slices) |
| ½ cup butter, softened |
| 2 cloves garlic, minced |

| **Recipe Yield** | **Prep Time** | **Total Time** |
| 12 servings | 10 minutes | 15 minutes |

Directions

Cut bread into 1-inch slices with a serrated knife. Place softened butter in a small bowl. Add minced garlic and mix with metal spoon until well blended. Using a butter knife, spread butter mixture onto both sides of bread slices. Grill over medium heat 1–3 minutes each side, until golden brown.

Nutritional Information (per serving): Calories 179.0; Total Fat 7.7g; Cholesterol 20.3mg; Sodium 54.6mg; Total Carbohydrates 24.2g (Dietary Fiber 1.0g); Protein 4.1g

Ham and Cheese Breakfast Croissants

Bonnie's husband, Steve, loves to make these for Saturday morning breakfasts!

6 large eggs
2 T. nonfat milk
½ t. salt
¼ t. pepper
¼ lb. deli ham, chopped into small pieces
6 mini croissants
¾ cup cheddar cheese, shredded

Recipe Yield

6 servings

Prep Time

20 minutes

Total Time

25 minutes

Directions

Beat eggs in a medium bowl with a whisk, then add milk, salt, pepper, and chopped ham. Pour egg mixture into a medium skillet and scramble over medium heat, removing from heat while eggs are still moist. Slice croissant in half. Spoon ¼ cup scrambled eggs onto the bottom half of croissant, sprinkle eggs with shredded cheese, then replace top half of croissant to form a sandwich. Repeat with remaining croissants. Place sandwiches on a cookie sheet. Bake in a 350 degree oven for 5–7 minutes, until cheese is melted.

Nutritional Information (per serving): Calories 282.0; Total Fat 17.0g; Cholesterol 285.0mg; Sodium 1156.7mg; Total Carbohydrates 15.5g (Dietary Fiber 1.0g); Protein 15.5g

One-Pan Baked Omelet

So good anytime—for company,
Sunday brunch, or "breakfast for dinner."

4 slices thick cut bacon (can be turkey bacon) or ¼ lb. sausage (pork, beef, or turkey)*
1 T. butter
½ cup red or yellow onion, diced
1 cup potatoes, diced small (Yukon gold works best)
2–3 T. diced green chiles (or 2 t. finely diced jalapeños)
6 large eggs
2 T. milk
1 t. salt
½ t. pepper
2 cups shredded cheese (sharp cheddar or cheddar jack), divided
chopped fresh parsley or sliced green onions for garnish/serving
bottled salsa or hot sauce for serving

*If using sausage: crumble the sausage into pan and sauté over medium-low heat until cooked through, stirring to break up pieces. Drain on paper towel, and continue with recipe directions.

Recipe Yield	**Prep Time**	**Total Time**
2 large servings or 4 medium servings	20 minutes	35 minutes

Directions

Preheat oven to 350 degrees. Cut bacon into 1-inch pieces. Using an 8-inch ovenproof skillet or sauté pan, sauté bacon over medium heat for 5–7 minutes. Stir occasionally and cook until browned and crispy. Drain bacon on paper towel and remove excess grease from the pan. Over medium low to medium heat, add 1 T. butter to the pan, followed by onion and potatoes; cook for about 10 minutes or until potatoes are tender and onion starts to brown. When potatoes are almost done, add green chiles and sauté for 30–60 more seconds.

While onion and potatoes are cooking, beat together eggs, milk, salt, and pepper in a medium bowl. Stir in 1 cup of the cheese. At this point, set aside about 2 T. of bacon for topping, and add remaining bacon to the cooked potato mixture. Pour the egg mixture over potatoes. Place pan in the oven and bake for 15–20 minutes, just until the omelet puffs and eggs are not quite done in the center. Sprinkle with remaining shredded cheese and bake for 1 minute more. Do not overbake, as eggs will continue to cook once removed from oven. Garnish with the reserved 2 T. bacon and a sprinkling of parsley or green onion, if using. Serve immediately with salsa or hot sauce, if desired.

Nutritional Information (per 1 large serving): Calories 523.7; Total Fat 35.1g; Cholesterol 349.7mg; Sodium 1467.3mg; Total Carbohydrates 22.6g (Dietary Fiber 2.5g); Protein 29.5g

Orange Cream Smoothies

Really good and good for you—low-cal,
high-protein for breakfast, lunch, or snack!

1–6 oz. container orange cream flavored yogurt (preferably Yoplait), frozen
½ cup orange juice
¼ cup low-fat milk
1 scoop (approx. 3–4 T.) whey protein powder (natural flavor)
3–5 ice cubes

Recipe Yield

1–16 oz. or 2–8 oz.
servings

Prep Time

3 minutes

Total Time

3–4 minutes

Directions

Place frozen yogurt in blender; add orange juice and milk. Cover and blend until mixture comes together. (You may need to turn off motor and stir once, adding just a little more juice or milk.) With motor running, add 1 scoop of protein powder and mix until well blended. Drop in 3–5 ice cubes and mix until blended and icy. Adjust ice according to desired consistency. Serve immediately.

Nutritional Information (per 16 oz. serving): Calories 340.0; Total Fat 2.5g; Cholesterol 15.0mg; Sodium 172.0mg; Total Carbohydrates 47.5g (Dietary Fiber 0.5g); Protein 28.0g

Tip

Keep containers of yogurt in the freezer so they are ready to go at any time. Using a pair of scissors, cut off the bottom rim of the yogurt container. Discard the bottom rim, peel off the foil top, and push the frozen yogurt into the blender.

Tip

This can be done with any of your favorite yogurt flavors. When fruit is in season, add ½ cup to the blender along with the yogurt, replacing the ½ cup orange juice with more milk instead. (Raspberry cream, blueberry cream, strawberry cream . . . whatever you like! Prepare as above with or without fruit.)

Piña Colada Smoothies

A refreshing summer smoothie with a Caribbean flair.

1½ cups pineapple juice
2 cups nonfat frozen yogurt
6 T. cream of coconut*
3 cups ice

fresh pineapple slices and/or maraschino cherries, for garnish

*Cream of coconut can be found in the beverage mixer section of the grocery store, perhaps near the club soda.

Recipe Yield	Prep Time	Total Time
8 6–oz. servings	10 minutes	10 minutes

Directions

Pour pineapple juice into blender. Add frozen yogurt, cream of coconut, and ice. Blend until ice is incorporated and well blended. Pour into serving glasses. Garnish with fresh pineapple slices and a maraschino cherry.

Nutritional Information (per 6 oz. serving): Calories 130.0; Total Fat 1.9g; Cholesterol 2.5mg, Sodium 36.1mg; Total Carbohydrates 25.8g (Dietary Fiber 0.4g); Protein 2.2g

Roasted Maple Bacon

You'll never go back to plain fried bacon again. It's the best way to prepare bacon for a brunch crowd.

¾ lb. regular or thick-cut smoked bacon (or turkey bacon)
¼ t. pepper (optional)
2 T. real maple syrup

Recipe Yield

4–6 servings

Prep Time

25 minutes

Total Time

25 minutes

Directions

Preheat oven to 400 degrees. Spray baking rack with cooking spray. Place rack on a rimmed baking sheet lined with foil; arrange bacon in a single layer on baking rack. Sprinkle lightly with pepper (if using). Bake for 15–20 minutes, until the bacon begins to brown. Remove the pan carefully from the oven; there will be hot grease in the baking sheet! Brush bacon slices with maple syrup and bake for another 5 minutes, turning bacon halfway through and brushing syrup on the other side, until bacon is a warm golden brown.

Nutritional Information (per 3 slices): Calories 213.0; Total Fat 9.4g; Cholesterol 16.2mg, Sodium 306.8mg; Total Carbohydrates 26.9g (Dietary Fiber 0.0g); Protein 5.8g

Scrumptious Baked French Toast

Make this delicious dish the night before.

1–1 lb. loaf French bread, cut in 1-inch slices on the diagonal (12–13 slices)

8 large eggs

2½ cups milk

1 cup half-and-half

½ t. cinnamon

2 t. vanilla

butter (or butter spray)

Topping

¾ cup butter (1½ sticks)

3 T. corn syrup

1⅓ cups brown sugar, packed

1 cup chopped pecans (optional)

Recipe Yield

10–12 servings

Prep Time

20 minutes

Total Time

60 minutes (plus overnight refrigerator time)

Directions

Generously butter a 9 x 13 baking dish. Arrange bread slices in bottom of dish in 2 layers, until all bread is used. In large mixing bowl, beat together the eggs, milk, half-and-half, cinnamon, and vanilla. Pour over bread slices. Cover with plastic wrap and refrigerate overnight.

Hint

Cinnamon bread (with or without raisins) may also be used.

When ready to bake, preheat oven to 350 degrees. While oven is heating, combine the topping ingredients in a small saucepan and cook over medium heat until bubbling. Pour topping evenly over the egg/bread mixture. Bake uncovered for 40–45 minutes or until the center is set. If edges start to brown too quickly, cover edges with foil strips. When done, remove from oven and cool slightly before serving.

Nutritional Information (per serving): Calories 391.0; Total Fat 20.2g; Cholesterol 187mg, Sodium 432mg; Total Carbohydrates 42.6g (Dietary Fiber 1.1g); Protein 9.8g

Spiced Apple Cider

Amazing served hot or cold!

Contributed by Lori Fox—Phoenix, Arizona

2–2-inch cinnamon sticks
1 t. whole allspice
12 whole cloves
⅔ cup brown sugar
2 qt. (8 cups) apple cider

Recipe Yield

8 servings

Prep Time

10 minutes

Total Time

1–2 hours

Directions

Place cinnamon sticks, allspice, and cloves in a cheesecloth sack; tie cheesecloth securely with kitchen twine. Pour apple cider into a slow cooker, then add cheesecloth bag of spices and brown sugar. Simmer in crockpot until heated through and to desired level of spiciness. Discard cheesecloth. Serve cider hot with a dash of nutmeg or cool, chill thoroughly, and serve over ice.

Nutritional Information (per 1 cup serving): Calories 187.0; Total Fat 0.4g; Cholesterol 0.0mg; Sodium 15.6mg; Total Carbohydrates 53.7g (Dietary Fiber 0.5g); Protein 0.2g

Swedish Blender Pancakes

A breakfast delight!

3 eggs
1¾ cups milk
1 cup flour
2 T. sugar
1 t. salt
1 T. oil

Recipe Yield

4 servings

Prep Time

20 minutes

Total Time

20 minutes

Directions

Place eggs and milk in a blender. Add flour, sugar, salt, and oil. Blend until mixture is smooth, much like crepe batter. Cook on a lightly greased griddle or skillet over medium heat. Pancakes should be very thin and delicate. Roll up pancakes and place on serving platter. To keep warm, place in a 200 degree oven; lightly cover with foil until ready to serve.

Serve pancakes with butter, syrup, jam, fruit, or powdered sugar.

Nutritional Information (per serving): Calories 265.3; Total Fat 8.0g; Cholesterol 145.6mg; Sodium 670.6mg; Total Carbohydrates 35.9g (Dietary Fiber 0.8g); Protein 10.9g

Sweet Breakfast Breads

This bread is like dessert! Perfect for breakfast, brunch, or an afternoon snack.

2¼ t. yeast (1 packet)

2¼ t. kosher salt

4 eggs, lightly beaten

¼ cup honey

¾ cup lukewarm water

¾ cup (1½ sticks) unsalted butter, melted

3¾ cups unbleached all-purpose flour

egg wash (1 egg beaten with 1 T. of water)

Recipe Yield

2 loaves, 6 servings each

Prep Time

20 minutes

Total Time

4 hours (includes rising, resting, and baking times)

Directions

Mix the yeast, salt, eggs, honey, and melted butter with lukewarm water in a 5-quart bowl.

Mix in flour using a heavy-duty mixer with dough hook or a wooden spoon just until combined. The dough will firm up when chilled; do not try to work with it without chilling. (Do not be concerned about lumps in the dough; they will disappear when baking.)

Cover and allow to rest at room temperature until dough rises and collapses, approximately 2 hours. Place dough, loosely covered, in refrigerator to chill (approx. 1 hour). Dough can be used as soon as it is chilled, or refrigerated in a covered (not airtight) container and used over the next 5 days.

On baking day: grease two 9 x 4 x 3 loaf pans. Dust the surface of dough with flour and cut in half. Dust one half with more flour and quickly shape into a ball by rotating in your hands and stretching the surface of the dough to the bottom on each side. Elongate the ball into an oval shape and place in prepared pan. Repeat with other half of dough. Allow to rest at room temperature for 1 hour and 20 minutes.

Twenty minutes prior to baking, preheat oven to 350 degrees. Using a pastry brush, brush the top of each loaf with egg wash. Place loaves near the center of the oven and bake for 35–40 minutes or until medium golden brown.

Variations: when shaping the dough, you may insert chocolate chips, sweetened cream cheese, or your favorite jam into the center of the loaf, then complete baking process as directed. This dough may also be made into smaller, individual-sized loaves, especially if you add filling. Baking time for smaller loaves is reduced to 18–25 minutes.

Nutritional Information (per serving): Calories 290.0; Total Fat 7.7g; Cholesterol 102.0mg; Sodium 460.0mg; Total Carbohydrates 36.3g (Dietary Fiber 1.3g); Protein 6.5g

Thai Chicken Wraps

*It's the kick of the peanut sauce
that gives these wraps their pizzazz!*

Chicken

2–3 cups shredded cooked chicken (may use rotisserie chicken)

2 T. soy sauce

2 T. peanut oil

Salad

4 cups fresh bean sprouts

1½ cups shredded or thinly chopped carrots

¾ cup chopped celery

2 cups iceberg lettuce, shredded

6 green onions, sliced at an angle

2 T. sesame seeds

2 T. sugar

¼ cup rice wine vinegar

¼ t. salt

Peanut Sauce

½ cup chunky peanut butter

¼ cup soy sauce

2 T. rice wine vinegar

½ t. cayenne pepper

¼ cup vegetable oil

6–12-inch tortilla wraps

Recipe Yield	**Prep Time**	**Total Time**
6 servings	30 minutes	30 minutes

Directions

Mix shredded chicken with soy sauce and peanut oil. Set aside.

Combine salad ingredients together in a bowl. Set aside.

To prepare peanut sauce: whisk together peanut butter, soy sauce, vinegar, and cayenne pepper. Add oil by whisking in a slow stream until totally mixed in.

Serve by piling ½ cup salad on tortilla, followed by chicken. Drizzle liberally with peanut sauce before rolling tortilla. Repeat with remaining tortillas. Slice each wrap in half at an angle and serve with fresh fruit.

Nutritional Information (per serving): Calories 217.0; Total Fat 15.8g; Cholesterol 7.3mg; Sodium 970.0mg; Total Carbohydrates 13.7g (Dietary Fiber 3.1g); Protein 8.2g

Vegetarian Chile Rellenos

A great brunch hot dish with a southwestern flair.

Contributed by Jodi Heiser—Highlands Ranch, Colorado

2–27 oz. cans whole green chiles, drained and divided

4 cups (1 lb.) Monterey jack cheese, shredded and divided

4 cups (1 lb.) cheddar cheese, shredded and divided

6 eggs, slightly beaten

1¼ cups skim milk

¼ cup flour

½ t. salt

½ t. pepper

Recipe Yield

12 servings

Prep Time

10 minutes

Total Time

55 minutes

Directions

Preheat oven to 350 degrees. In a 9 x 13 baking dish, spread one can green chiles to cover the bottom of the dish, flattening chiles with a spoon. Sprinkle approximately half of the Monterey jack cheese and then half of the cheddar cheese over chiles. Repeat with a second layer of chiles and cheeses.

In a medium bowl, mix together beaten eggs, milk, flour, salt, and pepper. Pour egg mixture over chiles and cheese. Bake uncovered for 45 minutes.

Nutritional Information (per serving): Calories 313.0; Total Fat 22.8g; Cholesterol 193.3mg; Sodium 650.5mg; Total Carbohydrates 5.9g (Dietary Fiber 0.1g); Protein 19.7g

Soups, Salads, and Sides

Cheesy Potato Casserole
Chilled Strawberry Soup
Chinese Chicken Salad
Classic Chicken Noodle Soup
Creamy Southwestern Tortilla Soup
Easy Spanish Rice
Effortless Vegetable Beef Soup
Fancy Sweet Potato Fries
Fresh Mozzarella and Tomato Salad
Glazed Snow Peas
Harvest Roasted Vegetables
Italian Chicken Pasta Salad
Lemon Cream Spinach Pasta Salad
On-the-Go Potluck Salad
Oven Roasted Potatoes
Pine Nut Couscous
Potato Soup Extraordinaire
Rosemary Vermicelli Sauté
Sassy Asparagus with Sesame Seeds
Spicy Black Bean Soup
Spinach Salad with Orange Poppy Seed
   Dressing
Sweet Corn with Flavored Butters
Walnut Spinach Salad

Cheesy Potato Casserole

A classic Midwest favorite.

Contributed by Shannon Butler—Mason, Ohio

1–32 oz. bag frozen potato hash browns (diced or cubed style)
2–10 oz. cans cream of celery soup
2–8 oz. tubs onion and chive cream cheese
2½ cups sharp cheddar cheese, shredded and divided

Recipe Yield

8 servings

Prep Time

20 minutes

Total Time

50 minutes

Directions

Preheat oven to 400 degrees. Microwave frozen hash browns in a medium bowl for 3–5 minutes, until thawed. In a separate large bowl, mix together soup and cream cheese, and microwave on high for 3–5 minutes until melted, checking every minute and stirring until smooth and well blended. Add potatoes and 1 cup cheese. Mix until potatoes are well coated. Pour into a 9 x 13 baking dish and bake uncovered for 30–35 minutes. Top with remaining cheese and bake an additional 5 minutes.

Nutritional Information (per serving): Calories 357.0; Total Fat 26.6g; Cholesterol 48.0mg; Sodium 845.0mg; Total Carbohydrates 33.7g (Dietary Fiber 3.1g); Protein 11.1g

Chilled Strawberry Soup

You will not believe how amazing this is . . .
serve as an appetizer or light dessert!

2½ cups sour cream
1 lb. fresh strawberries, washed and hulled
½ cup powdered sugar
¼ cup vanilla
¼ cup grenadine or raspberry syrup*
3 cups half-and-half

*Raspberry syrup can be found in the coffee flavoring section of the grocery store.

Recipe Yield

16 servings

Prep Time

15 minutes

Total Time

2 hours 15 minutes

Directions

Blend sour cream, strawberries, powdered sugar, vanilla, and grenadine in blender until smooth. Pour strawberry mixture into a large bowl. Add half-and-half and stir until well mixed. Cover and chill in refrigerator for 2–3 hours. Spoon into small fruit or soup bowls and garnish with fresh strawberry slices. Enjoy!

Nutritional Information (per ½ cup serving): Calories 175.0; Total Fat 12.8g; Cholesterol 32.6mg; Sodium 38.2mg; Total Carbohydrates 11.5g (Dietary Fiber 0.4g); Protein 2.6g

Chinese Chicken Salad

Always a requested favorite!

Salad

3–4 cooked chicken breasts, diced (or 3–4 cups rotisserie chicken, shredded)

1½ heads of lettuce (or assorted bagged greens like romaine or spinach)

3 stalks (about ¾ cup) green onions, sliced thin at an angle

½–¾ cup toasted almonds, slivered

¼ cup sesame seeds, toasted

Dressing

¼ cup sugar

2 t. salt

½ t. pepper

¼ cup vinegar

½ cup salad oil

Topping

2 cups fried chow mein noodles, purchased (optional)

Recipe Yield	**Prep Time**	**Total Time**
6 servings	20–25 minutes	30–40 minutes

Directions

For salad: shred meat into small pieces. In a small skillet, toast ¼ cup sesame seeds over medium heat for 1–2 minutes until golden brown. Wash lettuce and tear into small pieces or use bagged or pre-torn lettuce. Place all the salad ingredients in a large salad bowl and toss.

For dressing: measure the sugar, salt, pepper, vinegar, and salad oil into a tightly covered container. Close securely and shake dressing well until sugar is dissolved. Pour over salad just before serving. Toss to coat. Top with fried chow mein noodles, if using.

Nutritional Information (per serving): Calories 350.6; Total Fat 22.4g; Cholesterol 52.5mg; Sodium 818.3mg; Total Carbohydrates 15.4g (Dietary Fiber 3.8g); Protein 24.3g

Classic Chicken Noodle Soup

A great warm-up for your body and soul!

4 boneless, skinless chicken breasts
3 carrots, sliced
3 stalks celery, chopped
1 medium onion, chopped
¼ cup parsley, chopped
2 T. chicken bouillon granules
¾ t. salt
½ t. pepper
2 qt. water
8 oz. egg noodles

Recipe Yield

6 servings

Prep Time

15 minutes

Total Time

1 hour 25 minutes

Directions

Combine all ingredients except noodles in large stockpot. Bring to a boil, then reduce heat to simmer. Cover and continue simmering for 45 minutes. Remove chicken breasts. Return broth to boiling, then add noodles, reduce to medium heat, and simmer for 15–20 additional minutes or until noodles are tender. Shred chicken and add back into soup. Continue to simmer until chicken is heated through.

Nutritional Information (per serving): Calories 369.0; Total Fat 2.8g; Cholesterol 146.1mg; Sodium 805.5mg; Total Carbohydrates 32.5g (Dietary Fiber 2.7g); Protein 52.1g

Creamy Southwestern Tortilla Soup

*A crockpot full of chicken, cheese,
and comfort for your next gathering!*

	x3
1 red bell pepper, chopped	3
1 small tomato, diced	3
1–8 oz. can whole kernel corn, drained	3
3 boneless skinless chicken breasts, cut into strips	9
1–10 oz. can cream of chicken soup	3
1½ cups water	4½c
1 t. cumin	1T
½ t. coriander	1½t
½ t. garlic powder	1½t
½ t. chili powder	1½t
½ t. salt	1½t
1–4 oz. can diced green chiles, drained	3
¼ t. jalapeño pepper, chopped	¾t
2 corn tortillas, cut into strips ¼-inch wide	6
½ cup shredded cheddar cheese	1½c
¼ cup cilantro, chopped	¾c

Recipe Yield

4 servings

Prep Time

10 minutes

Total Time

4 hours 40 minutes

Directions

In a slow cooker, stir together bell pepper, tomato, corn, and chicken. In a small bowl, mix together soup, water, cumin, coriander, garlic powder, chili powder, salt, green chiles, and jalapeño pepper. Once well mixed, pour into crockpot over chicken mixture. Cover and cook on low until chicken is tender and cooked through, about 4–5 hours. Add tortilla strips, cheese, and cilantro, and continue cooking on low an additional 30 minutes. Serve immediately with additional cheese, if desired.

Freezing Instructions

To make this recipe x3 and freeze the extra meals, use the quantity table listed for the appropriate ingredient amounts. Follow directions above for preparing soup. Cool completely. Pour soup into freezer bags and freeze, using freezer bag method. To serve, thaw and heat until warmed through.

Nutritional Information (per serving): Calories 360.0; Total Fat 11.1g; Cholesterol 103.4mg; Sodium 1395.5mg; Total Carbohydrates 24.0g (Dietary Fiber 3.3g); Protein 42.6g

Easy Spanish Rice

One-dish wonder . . . pop it right in the oven!

Contributed by Beverly Garrison—Highlands Ranch, Colorado

1–10 oz. can Rotel tomatoes and green chiles
2 cups cheddar cheese, shredded
2 cups long grain rice (uncooked)
½ cup vegetable oil
1 cup canned sliced black olives, drained
3 cups water
½ cup onion, chopped
salt and pepper to taste

Recipe Yield

10–15 servings

Prep Time

10 minutes

Total Time

1 hour 10 minutes

Directions

Mix ingredients all together and place in a 9 x 13 baking dish. Bake at 350 degrees uncovered for 1 hour. Fluff with a fork and serve!

Nutritional Information (per serving): Calories 230.0; Total Fat 18.7g; Cholesterol 19.8mg; Sodium 400.3mg; Total Carbohydrates 9.5g (Dietary Fiber 0.4g); Protein 5.5g

Effortless Vegetable Beef Soup

This soup actually tastes like it has been cooking all day!

Contributed by Alivia Butler—Mason, Ohio

1 lb. ground beef, browned and drained
1–14.5 oz. can diced whole new potatoes, drained
1–14.5 oz. can sliced carrots, drained
1–14.5 oz. can cut zucchini with Italian style tomatoes
1–14.5 oz. can diced tomatoes with basil, garlic, and oregano
1–14.5 oz. can beef bouillon, double strength
½ can water (use bouillon can)
salt and pepper to taste

Recipe Yield	Prep Time	Total Time
8 servings	10 minutes	20 minutes

Directions

Combine all ingredients in a large stockpot. Bring to boil. Reduce heat and simmer 3 minutes. Season to taste with salt and pepper, and serve.

Nutritional Information (per serving): Calories 182.2; Total Fat 11.8g; Cholesterol 42.5mg; Sodium 73.4mg; Total Carbohydrates 7.6g (Dietary Fiber 1.4g); Protein 10.9g

Hint

All canned vegetables called for in this recipe can be found in the Del Monte brand.

Fancy Sweet Potato Fries

A delicious complement for burgers or steak.

3–4 medium sweet potatoes, peeled
2 T. olive oil
2 cloves garlic, finely chopped (optional)
1 t. coarse kosher salt
½–1 t. pepper

Recipe Yield

4–6 servings

Prep Time

15 minutes

Total Time

1 hour

Directions

Preheat oven to 425 degrees. Cut each potato into ½-inch thick slices. Cut each slice lengthwise into ½-inch strips, then place potatoes in a shallow bowl. Add oil, garlic, and a sprinkling of salt and pepper. Toss to coat.

Spread potatoes on a baking sheet. Bake in preheated oven for 30–45 minutes, depending on size of fries, or until potatoes are tender, turning once. Add more oil, salt, and pepper if needed.

Nutritional Information (per serving): Calories 131.3; Total Fat 5.6g; Cholesterol 0.0mg; Sodium 498.3mg; Total Carbohydrates 19.6g (Dietary Fiber 2.1g); Protein 2.0g

Fresh Mozzarella and Tomato Salad

A wonderful summer salad or elegant appetizer for your next dinner party.

Dressing

1 T. balsamic vinegar
¼ cup extra virgin olive oil
1 T. onion, minced
1 T. fresh basil, minced
¼ t. dried oregano
1 clove garlic, minced

4–6 tomatoes, sliced
2 oz. fresh mozzarella cheese

Recipe Yield	**Prep Time**	**Total Time**
6 servings	15 minutes	15 minutes

Directions

In small bowl, mix together dressing ingredients. Place sliced tomatoes in serving dish, then cover with dressing. Cut fresh mozzarella into cubes and place on top of tomatoes. Cover and chill. May be served immediately or stored in refrigerator for up to 24 hours.

Nutritional Information (per serving): Calories 132.0; Total Fat 11.2g; Cholesterol 5.5mg; Sodium 56.0mg; Total Carbohydrates 6.5g (Dietary Fiber 1.4g); Protein 3.4g

Glazed Snow Peas

The sweet way to enjoy snow peas!

2 T. butter
3 cups (8 oz.) fresh snow peas
¼ cup green onions, chopped
½ t. sugar
¼ cup water
¼ t. salt

Recipe Yield	Prep Time	Total Time
4 servings	12 minutes	10 minutes

Directions

Melt butter in a large skillet over medium-high heat. Add snow peas, green onions, sugar, and water. Cover and let simmer for two minutes, then uncover and boil until the water evaporates. Remove from heat and let stand for two more minutes. Season with salt and serve.

Nutritional Information (per serving): Calories 61.0; Total Fat 5.8g; Cholesterol 15.9mg; Sodium 81.1mg; Total Carbohydrates 2.2g (Dietary Fiber 0.6g); Protein 0.6g

Harvest Roasted Vegetables

Who knew vegetables could taste so incredible?

6 carrots, peeled and sliced into 2-inch pieces
3 onions (yellow or red), quartered or sliced into ½-inch rings
2 cups (1 lb.) broccoli, cut into large florets
1 cup (½ lb.) cauliflower, cut into large florets
1 lb. whole mushrooms, cut in half
4–5 medium potatoes (regular or sweet), cut into large, bite-size pieces
1–2 T. olive oil
½ t. kosher salt
¼ t. freshly ground pepper

Recipe Yield

6 servings

Prep Time

20 minutes

Total Time

60–80 minutes

Directions

Preheat oven to 400 degrees. Rinse and dry chopped vegetables. Using a large baking sheet or jelly roll pan, arrange vegetables in a single layer in pan. Drizzle olive oil over vegetables, then sprinkle with kosher salt and pepper. Toss vegetables until well coated, adding more oil, salt, and pepper if needed.

Place baking sheet on middle rack and roast until veggies are lightly browned and tender, about 40–60 minutes. Check the vegetables halfway through cooking time, turning once. Serve with your favorite meat entrée.

> **Hint**
>
> Any combination of seasonal vegetables may be used.

Nutritional Information (per serving): Calories 241.1; Total Fat 5.5g; Cholesterol 0.0mg; Sodium 276.9mg; Total Carbohydrates 43.6g (Dietary Fiber 10.3g); Protein 9.2g

Italian Chicken Pasta Salad

This chilled pasta salad gets rave reviews from Bonnie's Bunko buddies!

Contributed by Virginia Cebell—Bakersfield, California

Salad

1–12 oz. pkg. rotelle pasta, cooked al dente and drained
1–6 oz. jar marinated artichoke hearts, drained and chopped
1–7 oz. jar green olives with pimentos, drained and sliced
1 cup parmesan cheese, grated
1 green bell pepper, chopped
1 lb. fresh mushrooms, sliced
6 cups cooked chicken, cubed

Dressing

2 pkgs. ranch dressing mix
¼ cup water
½ cup vinegar
1 cup olive oil

Recipe Yield

12 servings

Prep Time

30 minutes

Total Time

1 hour 30 minutes

Directions

Mix all salad ingredients in a large bowl. In a separate bowl, combine dressing ingredients and mix well. Pour dressing over salad and toss. Cover and chill in refrigerator for at least an hour. Can also be made the night before and stored in refrigerator.

Nutritional Information (per serving): Calories 255.0; Total Fat 12.5g; Cholesterol 6.6mg; Sodium 414.2mg; Total Carbohydrates 28.2g (Dietary Fiber 2.4g); Protein 7.4g

Lemon Cream Spinach Pasta Salad

Chicken or cooked shrimp can also be added for a light main course dish.

1 T. olive oil
½ cup red onion, minced
2 cloves garlic, minced
1½ cups heavy cream (more if needed)
zest and juice of 2 lemons, divided
2 t. salt
1 t. pepper
1 lb. fusilli (or corkscrew) pasta
1–12 oz. bag baby spinach
½ cup freshly grated parmesan cheese, plus more for topping
1 pint grape or cherry tomatoes, halved

Recipe Yield	Prep Time	Total Time
4–5 servings	30 minutes	40 minutes

Directions

In a medium saucepan, heat olive oil over medium heat. Add red onion and garlic, and sauté for 1 minute. Add heavy cream, the zest and juice of one lemon, salt, and pepper. Bring to a boil, then lower heat and simmer for 15–20 minutes, until sauce starts to thicken.

Bring a large pot of water to a boil, then add 1 T. of salt and the pasta and cook according to the package directions, (approx. 12 minutes) stirring occasionally. Drain pasta and place back in pot. Immediately add the cream sauce and cook over medium low heat for 3 minutes, until most of the sauce has been absorbed into the pasta. Pour hot pasta into a large bowl; add spinach, parmesan, and tomatoes. Toss well, season to taste, and serve hot. Garnish with lemon zest.

For a more intense lemon taste, lightly squeeze remaining half of lemon over pasta before serving.

Nutritional Information (per serving): Calories 549.7; Total Fat 20.1g; Cholesterol 87.1mg; Sodium 225.0mg; Total Carbohydrates 76.6g (Dietary Fiber 4.7g); Protein 19.2g

On-the-Go Potluck Salad

A delicious portable salad for camping, picnics, or concerts in the park!

3 cups fresh corn kernels (or frozen, thawed)
2 cups grape or cherry tomatoes, halved
1 cucumber, chopped
⅓ cup chopped red onion
⅓ cup chopped bell pepper (green, yellow, or red)
1–2 avocados, cubed and tossed in a little lemon or lime juice

Dressing

¼ cup olive oil
2 T. balsamic vinegar
¼ t. salt
¼ t. cracked black pepper
1 pinch cayenne pepper

4 cups bagged lettuce, assorted kinds

Recipe Yield	**Prep Time**	**Total Time**
6 servings	20–25 minutes	35–40 minutes

Directions

Combine first 6 ingredients in a large bowl; toss gently. Combine dressing ingredients in a small bowl, stirring with a whisk. Drizzle dressing over corn mixture; stirring gently. Place lettuce on top of corn, but do not toss until just before serving.

For picnics, camping, or concerts in the park: layer corn mixture into pint jars or lidded containers and top with lettuce. When ready to eat, invert on plate to serve. Extra dressing may also be prepared and added if needed.

Nutritional Information (per serving): Calories 260.5; Total Fat 18.9g; Cholesterol 0.0mg; Sodium 118.8mg; Total Carbohydrates 23.1g (Dietary Fiber 3.5g); Protein 4.6g

Oven Roasted Potatoes

A perfect complement to your next steak dinner!

1 lb. unpeeled potatoes, quartered
olive oil spray
½ t. kosher salt
¼ t. coarse ground pepper
½ t. onion powder

Recipe Yield

4 servings

Prep Time

6 minutes

Total Time

50–55 minutes

Directions

Preheat oven to 425 degrees. Place quartered potatoes in a 9 x 9 baking dish. Spritz potatoes with olive oil spray. Sprinkle with salt, pepper, and onion power. Stir until potatoes are well coated. Bake in oven for 45–50 minutes, turning once, until potatoes are tender and browned.

Nutritional Information (per serving): Calories 195.0; Total Fat 3.6g; Cholesterol 0.0mg; Sodium 303.7mg; Total Carbohydrates 37.5g (Dietary Fiber 4.7g); Protein 4.3g

Pine Nut Couscous

A perfect side dish for Mediterranean cuisine.

¼ cup unsalted butter
¾ cup shallots, choppped
3 cups chicken broth
½ t. kosher salt
½ t. ground black pepper
1½ cups couscous
½ cup toasted pine nuts
¼ cup dried currants, dried cranberries, or dried cherries
2 T. fresh flat-leaf parsley, chopped*

*Fresh chopped mint can be substituted

Recipe Yield

4–6 servings

Prep Time

20 minutes

Total Time

20 minutes

Directions

Melt butter in a large saucepan. Add shallots and cook over medium-low heat for 3 minutes, until translucent. Add chicken broth, salt, and pepper and bring to a boil. Turn off the heat. Stir in couscous, cover pan, and set aside for 10 minutes. Add pine nuts, currants, and parsley, and fluff with a fork to combine. Serve hot.

Nutritional Information (per serving): Calories 226.4; Total Fat 11.3g; Cholesterol 29.2mg; Sodium 445.9mg; Total Carbohydrates 25.1g (Dietary Fiber 2.0g); Protein 6.4g

Potato Soup Extraordinaire

A satisfying bowl of comfort—or add chicken for a complete meal.

Contributed by Laura Beutler—Roann, Indiana

6 potatoes, peeled

water

3 T. butter

1 onion, diced

3 T. flour

2 garlic cloves, minced

4–5 cups chicken broth

1 cup heavy cream, half-and-half, or milk

½ t. salt

½ t. pepper

2 cups sharp cheddar cheese, grated and divided

2 green onions, sliced and divided

2 cups cooked chicken, diced or shredded (optional)

For Serving

Real bacon bits (precooked, packaged/bottled)

Recipe Yield	**Prep Time**	**Total Time**
6 servings	30 minutes	30 minutes

Directions

Cut potatoes into similar-sized pieces so that they will cook evenly. Place potatoes in medium pan with enough water to cover. Bring to a boil and cook until almost tender, approximately 9–12 minutes. Do not overcook, as potatoes will finish cooking in the soup.

While potatoes are cooking, melt butter in a large pot over medium heat. Add onion and cook until just tender. Add flour to onion and stir until all flour is absorbed and bubbly; add garlic and sauté for another 30 seconds. All at once, pour in 4 cups of chicken stock, whisking until mixed in. Let the stock mixture simmer until thickened, whisking occasionally.

Drain the potatoes and gently mix them into the chicken stock mixture. Add cream or milk and season with salt and pepper to taste. Simmer for another 5–7 minutes, until mixture thickens; remove soup from heat. If mixture is too thick, add additional chicken stock to thin. Stir in cooked chicken, if using.

Stir in 2 T. green onions and 1 cup of grated cheese a little at a time, stirring constantly until the cheese melts into soup, adding more cheese to desired taste. (Cheese may also be added individually to bowls.) Divide soup between bowls. Top with bacon bits and a sprinkling of sliced green onions. Serve with hot, crusty bread.

Nutritional Information (per serving, without chicken or bacon): Calories 406.0; Total Fat 20.8g; Cholesterol 65.7mg; Sodium 605.9mg; Total Carbohydrates 44.4g (Dietary Fiber 5.4g); Protein 12.8g

Rosemary Vermicelli Sauté

A fragrant blend of herbs and seasonings!

Contributed by Marcia Sunahara—Castle Rock, Colorado

6 oz. vermicelli
1 T. olive oil
½ yellow onion, sliced
1 cup (4 oz.) mushrooms, sliced
1 t. garlic, minced
1 T. fresh lemon juice
1–5 oz. package fresh baby spinach
¼ t. kosher salt
2 t. chopped fresh rosemary (or ½ t. dried)
3 T. pesto

Recipe Yield

4 servings

Prep Time

20 minutes

Total Time

20 minutes

Directions

In a large saucepan, bring water to boil; add vermicelli and cook according to package directions.

Heat olive oil in large frying pan over high heat. Add onion, mushrooms, and garlic. Cook, stirring constantly, until onion is softened and starting to turn brown, about 4 minutes. Add lemon juice, spinach, salt, and rosemary. Cook until spinach is slightly wilted, about 4 more minutes. Transfer to bowl.

Add cooked vermicelli to vegetable mixture. Stir in pesto, mix well, and serve.

Nutritional Information (per serving): Calories 206.0; Total Fat 3.9g; Cholesterol 0.0mg; Sodium 174.7mg; Total Carbohydrates 35.0g (Dietary Fiber 2.8g); Protein 3.5g

Sassy Asparagus with Sesame Seeds

Also great using sugar snap peas, broccoli, or edamame.

3 cups (1½ lbs.) fresh asparagus
1½ t. fresh ginger, grated
2 t. butter
1 t. sesame oil
½ t. salt
⅛ t. freshly ground black pepper
pinch cayenne pepper or red pepper flake
1 t. white sesame seeds, toasted
1 t. black sesame seeds

Recipe Yield

4 servings

Prep Time

20 minutes

Total Time

20 minutes

Directions

Cut off woody ends of asparagus and cook, covered, in a small amount of boiling, salted water for 3–5 minutes or until crisp-tender. Drain well. Transfer asparagus to a serving bowl; set aside.

In a small saucepan, cook ginger in hot butter over medium-low heat for 1 minute. Remove from heat. Stir in sesame oil, salt, and pepper. Pour butter mixture over hot asparagus; toss to coat. Sprinkle with sesame seeds and serve.

Nutritional Information (per serving): Calories 93.6; Total Fat 3.3g; Cholesterol 5.1mg; Sodium 447.4mg; Total Carbohydrates 15.4g (Dietary Fiber 3.1g); Protein 3.2g

Spicy Black Bean Soup

Two variations of this soup—smooth or chunky—you decide.

5–6 slices bacon
1 medium onion, chopped
2 cloves garlic, minced or pressed
2 cups chicken broth (low sodium)
1–10 oz. can Rotel tomatoes and green chiles
1 T. ketchup
1 t. Worcestershire sauce
1½ t. chili powder
1 t. ground cumin
2–15.5 oz. cans black beans, drained, but do not rinse
½ t. salt
¼ t. pepper
1 T. fresh lime juice

For Serving

cilantro, chopped
sour cream
flour tortillas for dipping
green onions, sliced
grated cheese

Recipe Yield

4–6 servings

Prep Time

15 minutes

Total Time

30 minutes

Directions

Cut bacon into small pieces and place in a heavy stockpot over medium heat. Cook bacon about 4 minutes. Add chopped onion and sauté for another 4 minutes, until onion begins to turn translucent. Stir in garlic and sauté until fragrant, about 1 minute more. Add all remaining ingredients except lime juice.

Bring soup to a boil, then reduce heat to a gentle boil and let simmer for about 10 minutes. Season with additional salt or pepper, if needed. While soup is simmering, prepare toppings for serving.

When soup is done, remove from heat. Squeeze fresh lime juice into soup and stir. To serve, ladle into bowls and garnish with prepared toppings.

For a more traditional, smooth-textured bean soup, follow these instructions. After soup has simmered, carefully ladle 2–3 ladles of soup at a time into a blender or food processor and cover. Puree soup until smooth. Repeat this until all soup is blended. Return soup to stockpot and reheat. Squeeze fresh lime juice into soup and stir; ladle into bowls and garnish with prepared toppings.

Nutritional Information (per serving): Calories 227.3; Total Fat 4.6g; Cholesterol 6.5mg; Sodium 1,112.2mg; Total Carbohydrates 35.7g (Dietary Fiber 10.1g); Protein 14.1g

Spinach Salad with Orange Poppy Seed Dressing

The blend of ingredients in this salad coupled with an orange-based dressing is just wonderful! A delicious meal in itself!

Salad

½ small cantaloupe, seeded

7 cups fresh spinach, torn

1 cup fully cooked lean ham, cubed

½ medium red onion, thinly sliced

½ cup pecan halves

1 T. butter

Orange-Poppy Seed Dressing

3 T. sugar

1½ t. finely shredded orange peel

2 T. orange juice

2 T. vinegar

1 T. finely chopped onion

⅛ t. pepper

⅓ cup canola oil

1 t. poppy seeds

Recipe Yield

4 main course servings or 12 side salads

Prep Time

25 minutes

Total Time

25 minutes

Directions

For salad: cut cantaloupe from rind and chop into small pieces (may also slice thin and use mini cookie cutter to cut cantaloupe into shapes). Toss cantaloupe with spinach, ham, and onion. Chill until ready to serve. Place pecan halves in nonstick skillet with butter over medium-high heat just until toasted. Remove and place on a plate to cool.

For dressing: in a food processor or blender, combine sugar, orange peel, orange juice, vinegar, chopped onion, and pepper. Cover and process or blend until combined. With food processor or blender running, slowly add canola oil in a steady stream through opening in the top. Continue to process until mixture is thickened. Stir in poppy seeds. Cover and chill salad dressing until needed, up to 1 week. Shake before using. To serve, toss salad with dressing and sprinkle with toasted pecans.

Nutritional Information (per main course serving): Calories 383.2; Total Fat 3.0g; Cholesterol 16.0mg; Sodium 429.0mg; Total Carbohydrates 20.8g (Dietary Fiber 3.3g); Protein 10.1g

Sweet Corn with Flavored Butters

Sure to complete your summer cookout.

| 8 ears fresh sweet corn |
| salt |
| water |

Recipe Yield

8 servings

Prep Time

20 minutes

Total Time

20–30 minutes, depending on if corn is boiled or grilled

Directions

Remove silk and husks from corn. Cook sweet corn in deep stockpot, with salt and enough water to cover corn while boiling. Cook for 5–8 minutes at a boil, then remove from heat. Don't overcook. Alternately, corn can be grilled in its husks over medium-low heat for 20–30 minutes, turning several times, until tender. To prepare corn for grilling, gently peel back husks and clean silk from corn, then replace husks and soak corn in water for 20–30 minutes before grilling. Serve with flavored butter.

Cheese Flavored Butter

| ½ cup butter, softened |
| 1 T. grated cheese (Romano or parmesan) |
| 2 t. finely chopped red onion |
| ½ t. paprika |
| ½ t. ground white pepper |

In a small bowl combine butter, cheese, onion, paprika, and white pepper. Stir until well combined. Cover and chill in the refrigerator for at least 1 hour or up to 24 hours before serving to allow flavors to blend. Serve butter at room temperature.

Nutritional Information (1 ear corn with 1 T. butter): Calories 218.6; Total Fat 16.1g; Cholesterol 41.3mg; Sodium 138.3mg; Total Carbohydrates 17.7g (Dietary Fiber 2.6g); Protein 3.5g

Lime-Pepper Butter

½ cup butter, softened
½ t. lime zest
1½ t. lime juice
⅛ t. red cayenne pepper

In a small bowl combine butter, lime zest, lime juice, and red pepper. Mix until well-combined. Cover and chill in the refrigerator for at least 1 hour or up to 24 hours before serving to allow flavors to blend. Serve butter at room temperature. Store any remaining butter in a tightly covered container in refrigerator for up to 3 days.

Nutritional Information (1 ear corn with 1 T. butter): Calories 213.6; Total Fat 16.4g; Cholesterol 40.7mg; Sodium 122.5mg; Total Carbohydrates 17.4g (Dietary Fiber 2.4g); Protein 3.1g

Walnut Spinach Salad

The last time Susie served this, her guest exclaimed, "This salad tastes way too good to be good for you!" We agree.

Walnuts

½ cup walnuts

¼ cup sugar

Dressing

¼ cup cider vinegar

½ cup canola oil

2 t. Dijon mustard

2 t. light brown sugar

2 T. sliced green onions

Salad

6 cups spinach leaves

4 oz. Swiss cheese, shredded

4 oz. cheddar cheese, shredded

½ cup bleu cheese

½ cup sweetened dried cranberries

2 slices bacon, cooked crisp, drained, and crumbled

Recipe Yield	**Prep Time**	**Total Time**
8 servings	20 minutes	25 minutes

Directions

Place walnuts and sugar in nonstick skillet over medium-high heat, stirring constantly, until sugar dissolves. Remove from heat and place on plate to cool. Set aside.

Combine dressing ingredients in a bowl and whisk together until sugar is dissolved. Refrigerate until ready to serve.

Just before serving, combine all salad ingredients together in a bowl. Sprinkle cooled walnuts over salad and toss with dressing.

Nutritional Information (per serving): Calories 380.0; Total Fat 30.6g; Cholesterol 35.6mg; Sodium 316.6mg; Total Carbohydrates 17.4g (Dietary Fiber 1.5g); Protein 11.7g

Pasta, Pasta

Chicken Fettuccine Alfredo

Creamy Lemon Pasta with Asparagus
and Peas

Four Cheese Baked Ziti

Garlic Shrimp with Angel Hair Pasta

Homestyle Mac & Cheese

Jack's Sausage and Vegetable
Fettuccine

Pasta Primavera Extraordinaire

Pasta Sauce Italiano

Penne with Pancetta, Spinach, and Buttery Crumb Topping

Tortellini with Spinach Walnut
Marinara

Tuscan Chicken

Chicken Fettuccine Alfredo

*An everyday gourmet meal your family
will ask for again and again!*

3 boneless, skinless chicken breasts
20 oz. fettuccine
½ cup butter
2 cups heavy cream
1⅓ cups freshly grated parmesan cheese
½ t. salt
¼ t. pepper

Recipe Yield

8 servings

Prep Time

20 minutes

Total Time

25 minutes

Directions

Grill chicken breasts over medium-high heat until done. Slice across the grain (½-inch thick slices).

While chicken is grilling, bring a large pot of salted water to a boil. Drop in pasta and cook according to package directions; drain.

For alfredo sauce, melt butter in a large saucepan or skillet. Add cream and bring just to a boil. Reduce heat and simmer for 5 minutes, stirring, then add parmesan cheese, salt, and pepper. Turn off the heat; leave pan on warm burner.

Pour alfredo sauce over cooked pasta. Top with sliced chicken breasts and sprinkle with extra parmesan cheese. Serve immediately.

Nutritional Information (per serving): Calories 502.0; Total Fat 21.6g; Cholesterol 80.7mg; Sodium 597.0mg; Total Carbohydrates 45.0g (Dietary Fiber 7.0g); Protein 29.0g

Creamy Lemon Pasta with Asparagus and Peas

A zesty pasta full of garden goodness!

3 boneless, skinless chicken breasts, cooked and sliced thin (optional)
8 oz. twisted pasta (such as fusilli)
1¾ cups asparagus, sliced (approx. 1½ inches long)
1 cup frozen peas
1 T. butter
2 cloves garlic, minced
½ cup vegetable broth
1 t. cornstarch
⅔ cup heavy cream
⅔ cup grated parmesan cheese, divided
2 T. fresh lemon juice (about 1 lemon)
½ t. salt
¼ t. black pepper
¼ t. cayenne pepper

Recipe Yield	**Prep Time**	**Total Time**
4 servings	25 minutes	35 minutes

Directions

If you choose to serve this dish with chicken, sauté or grill chicken breasts and slice thin.

Meanwhile, cook pasta according to package directions, adding sliced asparagus for last minute of cooking time. Place peas in colander and pour cooked pasta mixture over peas; set aside.

In a large nonstick skillet, melt butter over medium-high heat. Add garlic and sauté for 1 minute. Combine broth and cornstarch in a small bowl. Stir until well blended. Add broth mixture to garlic and bring to a boil. Cook 1 minute or until sauce begins to thicken, stirring constantly.

Remove from heat and stir in cream, ⅓ cup parmesan cheese, lemon juice, salt, pepper, and cayenne pepper. Add pasta mixture to cream sauce and toss gently to coat.

Top with chicken, if using, and remaining ⅓ cup parmesan cheese; serve immediately.

Nutritional Information (per serving, with chicken): Calories 472.7; Total Fat 12.0g; Cholesterol 98.3mg; Sodium 748.0mg; Total Carbohydrates 53.4g (Dietary Fiber 3.9g); Protein 38.0g

Four Cheese Baked Ziti

A cheese lover's delight.

3 cups marinara sauce
2 cups shredded mozzarella, divided
½ cup freshly grated parmesan cheese
¼ cup crumbled goat cheese
¾ cup shredded white cheddar cheese (regular or sharp)
1 t. salt
12 oz. ziti or penne pasta
3 T. olive oil
½ t. pepper
½ t. dried basil (or 1 T. fresh basil, chopped)
½ lb. Italian sausage (pork, turkey, or chicken), cooked (optional)

Recipe Yield   **Prep Time**   **Total Time**

6 servings   30 minutes   45 minutes

Directions

Preheat oven to 350 degrees. In a medium saucepan, bring marinara sauce to a simmer and keep heated. In a medium bowl, mix together 1 cup of mozzarella and the remaining cheeses. Set aside.

In a large pot, cook pasta in salted, boiling water until al dente (approx. 9–11 minutes). Drain, return hot pasta to pot and toss with olive oil, pepper, basil, and remaining 1 cup of mozzarella. Pour the heated marinara sauce over pasta and mix together (if using sausage, add with sauce). Pour pasta into 8 x 8 baking dish. Top with blended cheeses. Bake in oven for 15 minutes or until cheese is melted and slightly bubbly. Serve with hot garlic bread.

Nutritional Information (per serving, without sausage): Calories 342.3; Total Fat 16.9g; Cholesterol 35.7mg; Sodium 450.4mg; Total Carbohydrates 37.1g (Dietary Fiber 1.7g); Protein 13.0g

Garlic Shrimp with Angel Hair Pasta

Beautiful to serve, delightful to eat!

8 oz. angel hair pasta
¾ cup olive oil, divided
½ cup white onion, coarsely chopped
3 large cloves garlic, chopped
1 t. salt (kosher or sea salt)
½ t. ground black pepper
1 lb. uncooked jumbo shrimp, peeled and deveined

Recipe Yield

4 servings

Prep Time

15 minutes

Total Time

20 minutes

Directions

Cook pasta according to package directions.

Puree ½ cup olive oil, onion, garlic, salt, and pepper in a blender until smooth. Place shrimp in a small bowl and toss with seasoning mixture. Let shrimp marinate for 15–30 minutes at room temperature. Heat remaining ¼ cup olive oil in a large skillet over high heat. Add shrimp with marinade and sauté just until shrimp are opaque in center, about 4 minutes. Serve over pasta.

Nutritional Information (per serving): Calories 681.3; Total Fat 42.4g; Cholesterol 239.8mg; Sodium 423.9mg; Total Carbohydrates 44.9g (Dietary Fiber 1.5g); Protein 31.1g

Homestyle Mac & Cheese

Comfort food at its best!

½ lb. elbow macaroni

Sauce

3 T. butter

3 T. flour

1 T. dry mustard

pinch nutmeg

3 cups milk (whole, 1 percent, or 2 percent)

½ cup onion, diced fine (optional)

1 egg

12 oz. (approx. 3 cups) shredded cheese (sharp cheddar, or combination of cheddar and Gruyère)

1 t. kosher salt

¼ t. black pepper

1 cup shredded or diced rotisserie chicken (optional)

Topping

2–3 T. butter

1 cup panko* or regular breadcrumbs

*Panko breadcrumbs can be found in the Asian/ethnic aisles of most grocery stores or in larger quantities in Asian markets. Panko crumbs are much lighter than regular bread-crumbs and make a crunchier coating when baked or fried.

Recipe Yield	**Prep Time**	**Total Time**
6–8 servings	20 minutes	45–50 minutes

Directions

Preheat oven to 350 degrees. In a large pot of boiling, salted water, cook the macaroni al dente according to package directions.

For sauce: while pasta is cooking, in a large saucepan melt butter over medium heat. Whisk in flour, mustard, and pinch of nutmeg and cook, stirring constantly, until thickened. Immediately add milk and onion (if using) and whisk until smooth. Let mixture simmer on very low heat for 8–10 minutes, stirring occasionally. While mixture is simmering, break egg into a small bowl and beat with a fork. Add 1–2 T. hot milk mixture to the beaten egg and continue mixing until smooth. Set aside. When milk mixture is smooth and slightly thickened, add egg mixture and 2 cups cheese, stirring to incorporate. Season with salt and pepper.

Stir macaroni into cheese sauce and pour into a 2-quart baking dish. (If using chicken, stir in with macaroni.) Top with remaining cheese.

For topping: melt butter. Toss the panko or breadcrumbs in butter with fork to coat. Sprinkle evenly on top of macaroni. Bake for 30 minutes or until bubbly and golden brown on top. Let rest 5 minutes before serving.

Nutritional Information (per serving): Calories 506.4; Total Fat 27.3g; Cholesterol 116.6mg; Sodium 417.2mg; Total Carbohydrates 40.6g (Dietary Fiber 1.9g); Protein 24.6g

Jack's Sausage and Vegetable Fettuccine

A great blend of flavors . . . a true Italian comfort food!

12 oz. fettuccine
1 lb. Italian sausage
½ cup olive oil
12 large fresh mushrooms
2 cloves garlic
1 large green pepper, seeded and chopped
½ cup green onions, chopped
½ cup fresh parsley, minced
¼ cup fresh basil, chopped, or 2 t. dried basil
⅔ cup parmesan cheese, grated
1 cup sour cream

Recipe Yield

8 servings

Prep Time

25 minutes

Total Time

25 minutes

Directions

Cook fettuccine according to package directions; drain and set aside. In large skillet, cook sausage until brown. Remove sausage from skillet, drain, and set aside. Wipe excess grease from pan with paper towel.

Add olive oil to skillet and sauté mushrooms, garlic, green pepper, green onions, parsley, and basil over medium heat until tender. Stir in sausage. Place fettuccine in serving dish. Add sausage mixture, parmesan cheese, and sour cream. Toss gently and serve immediately.

Nutritional Information (per serving): Calories 590.0; Total Fat 40.7g; Cholesterol 62.1mg; Sodium 601.0mg; Total Carbohydrates 37.8g (Dietary Fiber 3.2g); Protein 19.2g

Pasta Primavera Extraordinaire

An easy and classic Italian dish.

10 oz. fettuccine
1 cup fresh broccoli florets
1 cup carrots, chopped
½ cup butter
2 cloves garlic, minced
1 cup half-and-half
1 cup chicken broth
1½ cups fresh parmesan cheese, shredded

Recipe Yield

6 servings

Prep Time

30 minutes

Total Time

30 minutes

Directions

Cook fettuccine in boiling water to al dente according to package directions. Drain pasta. Cook broccoli and carrots in microwave or steam in saucepan on stovetop until crisp-tender. Drain vegetables. In medium skillet, sauté garlic in butter until garlic is tender. Add half-and-half, then chicken broth. Heat until almost boiling. Add parmesan cheese, and continue stirring until cheese is melted and sauce is smooth. Add pasta and vegetables. Serve immediately. Garnish with extra parmesan cheese, if desired.

Nutritional Information (per serving): Calories 451.0; Total Fat 28.3g; Cholesterol 76.2mg; Sodium 769.8mg; Total Carbohydrates 34.0g (Dietary Fiber 2.4g); Protein 17.3g

Pasta Sauce Italiano

Authentic-tasting marinara sauce in a matter of minutes!

4–5 slices bacon or 6 oz. pancetta (Italian bacon)
1–2 T. olive oil
1 medium onion, finely chopped
2 cloves garlic, minced
¼ t. red pepper flakes, or ⅛ t. ground cayenne pepper
1 T. tomato paste
½ t. kosher salt
½ t. pepper
¼ cup dry red or white wine (optional)
1–28 oz. can crushed tomatoes
1 t. dried basil or 1–2 T. fresh basil, chopped
½ cup (1 oz.) Pecorino Romano, grated (or parmesan)

Recipe Yield

4–6 servings

Prep Time

20 minutes

Total Time

35 minutes

Directions

In a large skillet or Dutch oven, cook bacon in 1 T. oil over medium heat for 5–6 minutes or until golden brown. Remove bacon from skillet and set aside. In same skillet, add onion and sauté for 5–6 minutes; add garlic, red pepper flakes, tomato paste, salt, and pepper, and sauté for 30 more seconds, until fragrant. Add wine if using and cook, stirring constantly, for 1–2 minutes or until liquid has evaporated. Stir in crushed tomatoes, basil, and bacon. Simmer, partially covered, for about 20–25 minutes until the sauce thickens. Stir in Romano cheese. Taste and adjust seasonings, if needed. Add sauce to cooked pasta of your choice or Tender Baked Meatballs (see page 150). Top with additional cheese if desired and serve.

Nutritional Information (per serving): Calories 611.0; Total Fat 48.0g; Cholesterol 78.0mg; Sodium 898.0mg; Total Carbohydrates 13.4g (Dietary Fiber 3.1g); Protein 31.9g

Penne with Pancetta, Spinach, and Buttery Crumb Topping

A creamy, delicious side dish—or a meal in itself!

8 cups cooked penne pasta, drained
¾ cup (3 oz.) pancetta (Italian bacon), diced
¾ cup onion, chopped
2 t. garlic, minced
⅓ cup flour
3¾ cups 2 percent milk, divided
¼ cup half-and-half
6 cups fresh spinach, chopped
½ cup Parmigiano-Reggiano cheese, grated
1¼ t. salt
½ t. pepper
¾ cup breadcrumbs
¼ cup butter, melted

Recipe Yield

10 servings

Prep Time

25 minutes

Total Time

30 minutes

Directions

Preheat oven to 425 degrees. Heat a large nonstick saucepan over medium-high heat. Coat the pan with cooking spray. Add pancetta, onion, and garlic. Sauté five minutes or until onion is tender.

Lightly spoon flour into a dry measuring cup; level with a knife. Place flour in a small bowl; gradually add ¾ cup milk, stirring until smooth. Add flour mixture, remaining 3 cups milk, and half-and-half to pan; bring to a boil, stirring constantly. Reduce heat, and simmer for 2 minutes or until thick, stirring constantly. Add spinach and cook 1 more minute. Remove from heat. Stir in cheese, salt, and pepper, and continue stirring until cheese melts.

Place hot pasta in a large bowl. Add sauce to pasta; toss well. Spoon into a 9 x 13 baking dish coated with cooking spray. Sprinkle breadcrumbs over pasta, then drizzle melted butter on top of breadcrumbs. Bake at 425 degrees for 6 minutes or until lightly browned.

Nutritional Information (per serving): Calories 404.0; Total Fat 12.8g; Cholesterol 29.6mg; Sodium 714.0mg; Total Carbohydrates 56.0g (Dietary Fiber 3.04g); Protein 15.6g

Tortellini with Spinach Walnut Marinara

A vegetarian delight!

5 oz. frozen chopped spinach
1–24 oz. pkg. cheese tortellini
⅓ cup olive oil
1 cup chopped walnuts
2 cloves garlic, minced
30 oz. tomato sauce
1 T. fresh basil, chopped
½ t. salt
½ cup freshly grated parmesan cheese
toasted walnuts for garnish (optional)

Recipe Yield

12 servings

Prep Time

30 minutes

Total Time

35 minutes

Directions

Cook spinach according to package directions. Drain well. Cook tortellini al dente, according to package directions, and drain. In a medium saucepan, cook olive oil, chopped walnuts, and garlic over medium heat, until walnuts are lightly toasted. Add tomato sauce, spinach, basil, and salt, and continue cooking over medium heat until heated through. Place drained tortellini in a greased 9 x 13 baking dish. Cover with spinach marinara sauce and top with parmesan cheese. Place under oven broiler and broil for 3–5 minutes, until cheese is lightly golden. Garnish with additional toasted walnuts if desired.

Nutritional Information (per serving): Calories 263; Total Fat 17.5g; Cholesterol 15.8mg; Sodium 610.1mg; Total Carbohydrates 20.7g (Dietary Fiber 3g); Protein 8.7g

Tuscan Chicken

A taste of Tuscany!

3 cups uncooked penne pasta
1 lb. boneless, skinless chicken tenders
1 T. butter
1 cup chopped asparagus (can substitute broccoli)
8 oz. cream cheese
½ cup water
½ cup pesto
½ cup grated parmesan cheese, divided
1 cup cherry tomatoes

Recipe Yield

4 servings

Prep Time

20 minutes

Total Time

30 minutes

Directions

Cook pasta according to package directions. Meanwhile, heat chicken tenders in large skillet until cooked through (about 3–5 minutes per side). Remove chicken and set aside.

In same skillet, sauté asparagus in 1 T. of butter over medium heat until heated through. Add cream cheese and gently stir until mixed in and melted. Add water, pesto, ¼ cup parmesan cheese, and cherry tomatoes. Heat on medium until sauce is well blended and smooth. Return cooked chicken to pan and cover; cook on low heat for 2 minutes.

Serve over penne, and top with remaining parmesan cheese. This is especially delicious served with sourdough bread and a salad!

Nutritional Information (per serving): Calories 463.4; Total Fat 27.5g; Cholesterol 90.2mg; Sodium 438.2mg; Total Carbohydrates 35.0g (Dietary Fiber 2.9g); Protein 19.7g

Crockpot Collection

Asian Style Ribs

The orange marmalade is the secret ingredient in these ribs!

	x3
3 lbs. country style pork ribs	9 lbs
¼ cup soy sauce	¾c
¼ cup orange marmalade	¾c
2 T. ketchup	¼c + 2T
1 clove garlic, crushed	3

Recipe Yield

6 servings

Prep Time

10 minutes

Total Time

8–10 hours

Directions

Place ribs in crockpot. Mix remaining ingredients and pour over ribs. Cover and cook on low for 8–10 hours. These ribs are especially tangy and delicious when served with rice.

Freezing Instructions

To make this recipe x3 and freeze the extra meals, use the quantity table listed for the appropriate ingredient amounts. Place ribs in freezer bag. Mix remaining ingredients and pour over ribs. Freeze, using freezer bag method. On serving day, thaw and cook as directed.

Nutritional Information (per serving): Calories 717.0; Total Fat 48.7g; Cholesterol 197.2mg; Sodium 786.9mg; Total Carbohydrates 11.5g (Dietary Fiber 0.2g); Protein 54.8g

Cajun Brisket

Tender brisket with a spicy kick.

Contributed by Jeanie Wilking—Lakewood, Colorado

1–12 oz. jar jalapeño peppers (not pickled), drained and sliced
3 lbs. beef brisket
3 T. Cajun spice blend
2 onions, sliced
¼ cup brown sugar, packed
3–10 oz. cans beef broth (low sodium)
hot water

Recipe Yield	Prep Time	Total Time
6–8 servings	20 minutes	5–6 hours

Directions

Layer half of the jalapeño peppers in crockpot; place brisket on top of peppers and sprinkle the entire top of the brisket with Cajun Spice blend. Layer remaining peppers on top of beef, followed by onions. Mix brown sugar into one of the cans of beef broth and stir to dissolve. Pour all of the broth gently over brisket. Add enough water so that the liquid in crockpot is about 1–1½ inches above the meat.

Cover crockpot and cook on high for 5–6 hours. Remove meat when tender. Remove fat, then shred meat and place in large serving bowl. Add enough juices from crockpot to keep meat moist and mix well.

Serve shredded meat with potatoes, or on sandwich rolls with a slice of melted cheddar cheese.

Nutritional Information (per serving): Calories 380.0; Total Fat 18.3g; Cholesterol 101.1mg; Sodium 643.0mg; Total Carbohydrates 15.2g (Dietary Fiber 1.1g); Protein 43.7g

Chicago Style Beef Sandwiches

Just like you buy at the sandwich stand on the streets of Chicago!

Contributed by Donna Mayberry—Denver, Colorado

	x3
4 lbs. boneless rump roast	12 lbs
2 pkgs. Italian dressing mix	6
2 cups water	6c
1–16 oz. jar mild pepper rings, undrained	3
Serving Day	
18 hoagie buns, split	54

Recipe Yield	**Prep Time**	**Total Time**
18 servings	10 minutes	8 hours, 10 minutes

Directions

Place roast in crockpot. In a separate bowl, mix together water and Italian salad dressing mix, then pour over roast. Cover and cook on low for 8 hours, until meat is tender. Remove meat and shred with two forks. Return to crockpot and add pepper rings. Continue cooking on low until heated through. To serve, toast hoagie rolls in cast iron skillet or under broiler, then spoon ½ cup of meat mixture onto each roll.

Freezing Instructions

To make this recipe x3 and freeze the extra meals, use the quantity table listed for the appropriate ingredient amounts. Cook in crockpot as directed. Once meat is cooked and peppers added, cool completely. Spoon meat into freezer bags in serving size portions. Freeze, using freezer bag method. On serving day, thaw and reheat on stovetop or in microwave.

Nutritional Information (per ½ cup serving of meat): Calories 234.0; Total Fat 13.8g; Cholesterol 48.9mg; Sodium 630.7mg; Total Carbohydrates 4.3g (Dietary Fiber 0.3g); Protein 18.8g

Chicken Brunswick Stew

A southern homestyle stew your family will love.

Contributed by Susan Jones—Englewood, Colorado

1 onion, chopped

6 boneless, skinless chicken breast halves

2–15 oz. cans cream-style corn

1–28 oz. can crushed tomatoes

1–12 oz. bottle chili sauce

2–14.5 oz. cans chicken broth

¼ cup Worcestershire sauce

¼ cup butter, cubed

2 T. cider vinegar

2 t. dry mustard

½ t. salt

½ t. pepper

½ t. hot pepper sauce

Recipe Yield	**Prep Time**	**Total Time**
8–10 servings	30 minutes	4½ hours

Directions

Place chopped onion in bottom of crockpot. Place chicken breasts over onion. Spoon creamed corn over chicken. Mix together remaining ingredients in medium bowl, then pour into crockpot. Cover and cook on high for 4 hours or until chicken is tender. Remove chicken, shred, then return to stew. Serve immediately.

Nutritional Information (per serving): Calories 234.0; Total Fat 5.0g; Cholesterol 68.7mg; Sodium 911.7mg; Total Carbohydrates 23.0g (Dietary Fiber 1.0g); Protein 24.9g

Flank Steak in Mushroom Sauce

This fork-tender steak will melt in your mouth.

1½ lbs. flank steak
¼ cup sauterne or similar sweet wine
1 T. soy sauce
1 T. ketchup
1 t. mustard
1 T. dried minced onion
1 clove garlic, minced
1–10 oz. can beef broth
¼ cup cornstarch
¼ cup water
¼ lb. sliced fresh mushrooms

Recipe Yield

4–6 servings

Prep Time

15 minutes

Total Time

7–9 hours

Directions

Place flank steak in crockpot. Combine wine, soy sauce, ketchup, mustard, onion, garlic, and broth. Pour over steak. Cover and cook on low for 6–8 hours. In a small bowl, dissolve cornstarch in water. Stir into crockpot. Add mushrooms. Turn crockpot to high and continue cooking for an additional 30 minutes. Lift meat from crockpot onto platter. Spoon juices over meat and cut into serving size pieces.

Nutritional Information (per serving): Calories 214.0; Total Fat 8.6g; Cholesterol 56.7mg; Sodium 430.4mg; Total Carbohydrates 6.7g (Dietary Fiber 0.2g); Protein 24.1g

French Dip Sandwiches

The au jus for dipping makes this sandwich a hit!

1 rump roast, about 2½ lbs.
½ t. salt
¼ t. pepper
2 T. oil
1–10 oz. can beef broth
1 pkg. onion soup mix

For Serving

10 hoagie rolls, toasted
10 slices provolone cheese (optional)

Recipe Yield	Prep Time	Total Time
10 servings	15 minutes	4–5 hours

Directions

Heat oil in nonstick skillet. Sprinkle roast with salt and pepper, then brown all sides in oil (3–5 minutes). Pour beef broth in crockpot and stir in onion soup mix. Place browned roast in crockpot. Cook on low for 4–5 hours.

Remove roast from crockpot and allow to rest for a few minutes while preparing rolls.

Slice rolls in half lengthwise. Butter inside of rolls and place on cookie sheet under broiler (watching very closely) until lightly browned.

Slice roast very thin and place on prepared rolls. If desired, top meat with provolone cheese and return to broiler until cheese is melted. Pour au jus from crockpot into small dipping bowls. Enjoy!

Nutritional Information (per serving, with cheese): Calories 612.0; Total Fat 25.7g; Cholesterol 121.0mg; Sodium 443.0mg; Total Carbohydrates 34.7g (Dietary Fiber 2.6g); Protein 49.0g

Heidi's Pulled Pork

Great for crowds large or small.

Contributed by Heidi Messer—Denver, Colorado

1 bone-in pork shoulder roast, about 3 lbs.
1 whole orange
1–18 oz. bottle hickory-smoked barbecue sauce

For Serving

12 buns or rolls

Recipe Yield

12 servings

Prep Time

10 minutes

Total Time

5–6 hours

Directions

Place roast in crockpot. Cut orange in half and squeeze juice from both halves over the roast, then place orange in crockpot. Spoon half the bottle of barbecue sauce over meat. Cover crockpot and cook on high for 4 hours or low for 6 hours, until roast is tender. Remove roast from crockpot and place meat on a large plate or pan. Remove bone and orange and discard. Using two forks, shred the pork into long strips, then place meat back in crockpot. Add remaining barbecue sauce and stir. Cover and continue cooking on low for an additional 30–60 minutes. Place meat on toasted buns and enjoy!

Nutritional Information (per serving): Calories 519.0; Total Fat 27.2g; Cholesterol 106.5mg; Sodium 362.7mg; Total Carbohydrates 40.6g (Dietary Fiber 0.2g); Protein 12.8g

Honey Curry Chicken

Even if you don't like curry, you will like this dish.

	x3
6 boneless, skinless chicken breasts	18
¼ cup butter	¾c
½ cup honey	1½c
1 t. mustard	1T
1 t. salt	1T
1 t. curry powder	1T

Recipe Yield	Prep Time	Total Time
6 servings	15 minutes	3–5 hours

Directions

Place chicken breasts in crockpot. In a medium skillet, melt butter. Add honey, mustard, salt, and curry powder to melted butter, and stir until well blended. Pour butter mixture over chicken breasts, turning chicken to coat. Cover crockpot and cook on high for 3 hours or low for 5 hours, until chicken is tender. Serve with rice.

Freezing Instructions

To make this recipe x3 and freeze the extra meals, use the quantity table listed for the appropriate ingredient amounts. Place chicken in freezer bags. Mix remaining ingredients and pour over chicken. Freeze, using freezer bag method. On serving day, thaw and cook in crockpot as directed.

Nutritional Information (per serving): Calories 355.0; Total Fat 8.7g; Cholesterol 130.3mg; Sodium 912.7mg; Total Carbohydrates 23.5g (Dietary Fiber 0.2g); Protein 46.2g

Lemon Chicken

A go-to recipe for your crockpot repertoire!

6 boneless, skinless chicken breasts
1 t. dried oregano
½ t. salt
¼ t. ground black pepper
2 T. butter
¼ cup water
3 T. fresh lemon juice
2 cloves garlic, minced
1 t. chicken bouillon granules
1 T. fresh parsley, chopped

Recipe Yield

6 servings

Prep Time

20 minutes

Total Time

3–5 hours

Directions

In a small bowl, mix oregano, salt, and pepper. Rub the mixture into chicken. Melt butter in a skillet over medium heat. Brown seasoned chicken in butter for 3–5 minutes on each side. Place chicken in crockpot.

In the same skillet, mix water, lemon juice, garlic, and bouillon. Bring the mixture to a boil, then pour over chicken in crockpot. Cover and cook on high for 3 hours or low for 5 hours. Add parsley to crockpot for the last 15–30 minutes of cook time. Serve with rice or pasta and a fresh salad!

Nutritional Information (per serving): Calories 193.0; Total Fat 7.0g; Cholesterol 88.0mg; Sodium 430.0mg; Total Carbohydrates 21.2g (Dietary Fiber 6.3g); Protein 19.6g

Shredded Beef Burritos

This can also be used as filling for chimichangas, enchiladas, or soft tacos.

Contributed by Paula Rome—Lone Tree, Colorado

	x3
2 lbs. boneless beef chuck or pot roast	6 lbs
1 jalapeño pepper, seeded and chopped	3
1 clove garlic, minced	3
1 beef bouillon cube	3
1 onion, chopped	3
½ t. chili powder	1½t
½ t. cumin	1½t
2 T. cilantro, chopped	¼c + 2T
½ t. salt	1½t

1–16 oz. can refried beans, heated
6–8 12-inch flour tortillas, warmed

Recipe Yield

6–8 servings

Prep Time

20 minutes

Total Time

8 hours 20 minutes

Directions

Trim fat from beef and discard. In a crockpot, combine meat, jalapeño, garlic, bouillon cube, onion, chili powder, cumin, cilantro, and salt. Cover and cook on low for 8 hours or until meat is very tender. Remove meat from crockpot and shred with two forks; combine with ¾ cup cooking juices. To serve, spread warm tortillas with refried beans. Add shredded beef. Wrap tortillas burrito style. Add favorite toppings and serve.

Freezing Instructions

To make this recipe x3 and freeze the extra meals, use the quantity table listed for the appropriate ingredient amounts. Follow directions above for cooking instructions. Once shredded beef is cool, place in freezer bags. Freeze, using freezer bag method. To serve, thaw and heat through on stovetop or in microwave.

Nutritional Information (per serving of meat): Calories 344.0; Total Fat 22.1g; Cholesterol 68.0mg; Sodium 331.7mg; Total Carbohydrates 1.5g (Dietary Fiber 0.3g); Protein 32.3g

Shredded Pork Soft Tacos

Your family will think you fussed all day on this meal!

Contributed by Beverly Garrison—Highlands Ranch, Colorado

Meat

3 lbs. country-style pork ribs
1 T. oregano
1 T. coarsely ground pepper
2 t. kosher salt

Tacos

flour or corn tortillas, warmed
tomatillo salsa (a green salsa that goes great with pork)
lettuce
tomato
cheese
sliced avocado

Recipe Yield
8–10 servings

Prep Time
5 minutes

Total Time
6–8 hours

Directions

Place ribs in crockpot. Sprinkle seasonings over meat. Cover and cook on low for 6–8 hours, until meat is tender and can be shredded with two forks. Remove bones and extra fat from meat.

Assemble soft tacos using tortillas, salsa, and favorite toppings.

Hint

No extra liquid is needed when cooking these ribs!

Nutritional Information (per serving of meat): Calories 406.0; Total Fat 29.3g; Cholesterol 118.3mg; Sodium 545.7mg; Total Carbohydrates 0.7g (Dietary Fiber 0.4g); Protein 32.6g

Slow Cooker Coq au Vin

A delicious, easy version of classic French chicken and wine.

8 (3½ lbs.) boneless, skinless chicken pieces (thighs and breasts)
¾ t. salt
½ t. pepper
4–5 slices bacon, cut into 1-inch pieces
10 oz. whole mushrooms, quartered
2 cups pearl onions, frozen
2 medium onions, diced
1 large carrot, sliced
olive oil, for sautéing
3 cloves garlic, diced
2 bay leaves
2 T. tomato paste
1½–2 cups dry red wine
1 cup chicken broth

Recipe Yield	**Prep Time**	**Total Time**
4–6 servings	30 minutes	4–8 hours

Directions

Season chicken pieces with salt and pepper; set aside. In a large nonstick skillet, cook bacon pieces over medium heat until browned and crisp. Transfer bacon to paper towels to drain. Set aside until serving time.

In the same skillet, brown chicken over medium heat, about 5 minutes per side. This may take two batches. While chicken is cooking, place mushrooms and pearl onions in crockpot. Layer browned chicken on top of onions and mushrooms.

In the same pan, sauté diced onions and carrots over medium heat, stirring frequently. Add olive oil as needed and cook until onions are soft, about 2 minutes; add garlic and sauté for 1 minute more. To this mixture add bay leaves, tomato paste, wine, and chicken broth. Heat to boiling, stirring, until tomato paste dissolves. Carefully pour this mixture over the chicken pieces. Cover and cook on high for 4 hours or on low for 8 hours.

To serve, discard bay leaves. Crumble bacon into small pieces. Place chicken and sauce in large serving bowl, and sprinkle with bacon pieces. This is wonderful served with a side of mashed potatoes.

Nutritional Information (per serving): Calories 285.0; Total Fat 21.4g; Cholesterol 31.9mg; Sodium 429.0mg; Total Carbohydrates 9.4g (Dietary Fiber 1.8g); Protein 14.1g

Slow Cooker Pork Chops

A great meal to come home to after a long day at work.

Contributed by Cathy Healy—Castle Pines North, Colorado

1 onion, sliced
4–6 bone-in pork chops
½ cup apple juice
1–10 oz. can cream of mushroom soup
1 clove garlic, minced
½ t. pepper
1 t. thyme
1 cup fresh mushrooms, sliced

Recipe Yield

4–6 servings

Prep Time

5 minutes

Total Time

4 hours

Directions

Place sliced onion in bottom of crockpot. Layer pork chops on top of onion. Mix together all remaining ingredients except mushrooms and pour over pork chops. Cook on high for 4 hours. Place fresh mushrooms on top of pork chops during last hour of cooking time. Delicious served over rice or with noodles.

Nutritional Information (per serving): Calories 269.0; Total Fat 14.9g; Cholesterol 71.4mg; Sodium 378.8mg; Total Carbohydrates 8.2g (Dietary Fiber 0.6g); Protein 24.7g

Succulent Teriyaki Chicken

A crockpot version of a classic dish.

3½ lbs. boneless, skinless chicken breasts

¼ cup brown sugar, packed

¼ cup soy sauce

3 T. lemon juice

3 T. water

1 clove garlic, minced

½ t. ground ginger

¼ cup flour

¼ cup cold water

Recipe Yield

8 servings

Prep Time

15 minutes

Total Time

4 hours 15 minutes

Directions

Place chicken breasts in crockpot. Mix together brown sugar, soy sauce, lemon juice, 3 T. water, garlic, and ginger; pour over chicken breasts. Cover and cook on high for 4 hours, until chicken is tender. Pour juices from chicken into a medium saucepan. In a separate small bowl, mix together flour and cold water until smooth, then whisk into juices in saucepan. Cook on medium heat until sauce is thickened and smooth. Pour over chicken in crockpot and heat on low until warmed through. Serve with rice.

Nutritional Information (per serving): Calories 222.0; Total Fat 0.9g; Cholesterol 96.3mg; Sodium 854.8mg; Total Carbohydrates 13.5g (Dietary Fiber 0.2g); Protein 41.2g

Easy Baked Oven Dishes

Apricot Chicken
Chicken Divan
Easy Oven Barbecued Chicken
Garlic-Roasted Chicken
Gorgonzola Pinwheel Flank Steak
Hearty Oven Beef Stew
Honey Glazed Pork Tenderloin
Italian Chicken
New Orleans Style Shrimp Packets
One-Dish Dijon Chicken and Roasted
    Potatoes
Oven Roasted Orange Chicken
Regal Pork Roast
Rosemary Chicken with Shallots and
    Sweet Potatoes
Sesame Chicken with Hoisin Dipping
    Sauce
Shirley's Mini Meatloaves
Tender Baked Meatballs

Apricot Chicken

Always a favorite of kids and adults alike.

	x3
8 oz. Catalina or French dressing	24oz
1–1 oz. pkg. onion soup mix	3
1 cup apricot preserves	3c
2 T. green onion, thinly sliced	¼c + 2T
⅛ t. ground red pepper	⅜t
6 boneless, skinless chicken breasts	18

Recipe Yield

6 servings

Prep Time

15 minutes

Total Time

1 hour 15 minutes

Directions

Preheat oven to 350 degrees. In a medium bowl mix together dressing, soup mix, apricot preserves, green onions, and red pepper.

Place chicken pieces in a 9 x 13 baking dish. Pour apricot mixture over chicken and bake uncovered for 45–60 minutes, just until chicken is done. Do not over-cook. (Chicken continues to cook after removing from oven.)

Freezing Instructions

To make this recipe x3 and freeze the extra meals, use the quantity table listed for the appropriate ingredient amounts. Place chicken and apricot mixture together in a freezer bag. Freeze using freezer bag method. On serving day, thaw and bake as directed.

Nutritional Information (per serving): Calories 516.0; Total Fat 18.5g; Cholesterol 136.9mg; Sodium 754.8mg; Total Carbohydrates 26.7g (Dietary Fiber 0.4g); Protein 55.0g

Chicken Divan

A never-fails-to-please traditional favorite.

2 cups fresh broccoli

Sauce

¼ cup butter

⅓ cup flour

⅛ t. ground nutmeg

½ t. salt

⅛ t. pepper

1 cup milk, whole or 2 percent

1 cup chicken broth

¼ cup dry white wine

⅓ cup Swiss cheese, shredded

2 boneless, skinless chicken breasts, cooked and sliced

¼ cup grated parmesan cheese

1 t. paprika

Recipe Yield   **Prep Time**   **Total Time**

6 servings   20 minutes   45 minutes

Directions

Preheat oven to 350 degrees. Steam broccoli until crisp-tender. Arrange broc-coli in an even layer on bottom of a 9 x 13 baking dish.

For sauce: melt butter in a medium saucepan over medium heat, then stir in flour, nutmeg, salt, and pepper. Add milk and broth all at once. Cook and stir until bubbly, then continue to cook 1–2 minutes more. Stir in wine. Add Swiss cheese and stir just until melted.

Pour half of sauce over broccoli, then top with sliced chicken. Pour remaining sauce over chicken. Sprinkle parmesan and paprika on the top. Bake uncovered for 20 minutes or until heated through, then broil 3–4 inches from heat for up to 2 minutes or until golden brown.

Nutritional Information (per serving): Calories 276.0; Total Fat 13.0g; Cholesterol 57.2mg; Sodium 430.0mg; Total Carbohydrates 21.2g (Dietary Fiber 6.3g); Protein 19.6g

Easy Oven Barbecued Chicken

*You can serve crispy barbecued chicken
even in the middle of winter!*

8–10 pieces cut-up chicken
1 T. kosher salt
1 T. coarsely ground pepper
1 onion, sliced
2 cups barbecue sauce

Recipe Yield

8–10 servings

Prep Time

15 minutes

Total Time

1 hour 5 minutes

Directions

Mix kosher salt and pepper together in a small bowl. Rub onto all sides of chicken pieces and place chicken in a shallow baking pan. Place sliced onion on top of chicken pieces.

Bake at 425 degrees for 10 minutes. Decrease oven temperature to 350 degrees and continue baking for 30 minutes. Brush chicken pieces with barbecue sauce. Bake an additional 10 minutes. Turn chicken and coat again with barbecue sauce, then bake 10 more minutes. Baste chicken once more with barbecue sauce and broil on high, skin side up, for 2–3 minutes.

Nutritional Information (per serving): Calories 300.0; Total Fat 18.5g; Cholesterol 120.0mg; Sodium 1889.8mg; Total Carbohydrates 9.4g (Dietary Fiber 1.0g); Protein 26.7g

Garlic-Roasted Chicken

*The aroma of garlic and rosemary
will entice your family to the table!*

2 T. extra virgin olive oil
4 skin-on boneless chicken breasts
1 t. salt
½ t. pepper
2 heads garlic
4 sprigs fresh rosemary
4 slices sourdough bread, grilled or toasted
2 T. white wine vinegar

Recipe Yield

4 servings

Prep Time

15 minutes

Total Time

30 minutes

Directions

Preheat oven to 425 degrees. Heat olive oil in a large ovenproof skillet over medium-high heat. Season the chicken with salt and pepper and cook in skillet, skin side down, until browned, about 5 minutes. Separate the heads of garlic into cloves but do not peel. Flip the chicken over, add the garlic and rosemary to skillet, and transfer to the oven. Roast until chicken is cooked through but still moist, 15–20 minutes.

Place toasted bread on a platter and top each slice with a chicken breast. Return skillet to stovetop. Add vinegar to skillet and scrape up any browned bits with a wooden spoon. Add 3 T. water and simmer on stovetop until the sauce thickens slightly, about 2 minutes. Pour the sauce over the chicken and serve.

Nutritional Information (per serving): Calories 404.0; Total Fat 23.0g; Cholesterol 109.0mg; Sodium 234.0mg; Total Carbohydrates 10.0g (Dietary Fiber 2.0g); Protein 37.0g

Gorgonzola Pinwheel Flank Steak

Serve all year . . . simple yet fancy!

2 lbs. flank steak, pounded to ¼-inch thickness
½ t. garlic salt
¼ t. pepper
2 cups fresh spinach leaves
½ cup gorgonzola cheese

Recipe Yield

8 servings

Prep Time

20 minutes

Total Time

35 minutes

Directions

Pound flank steak with meat mallet into a rectangle ¼-inch thick. Sprinkle steak with garlic salt and pepper. Place an even layer of fresh spinach leaves over steak. Sprinkle with gorgonzola cheese, leaving a 1-inch border around the edges.

Roll up meat lengthwise, tightly, until you form a pinwheel. Tie the pinwheel with string at 1-inch intervals. Cut steak between strings to form individual pinwheel steaks. Broil steaks on high until desired doneness is reached, approximately 4 minutes per side.

Serve with potatoes and a fresh salad.

Nutritional Information (per serving): Calories 215.0; Total Fat 11.5g; Cholesterol 66.7mg; Sodium 222.0mg; Total Carbohydrates 1.2g (Dietary Fiber 0.3g); Protein 25.6g

Hearty Oven Beef Stew

A delicious, classic winter meal.

2 lbs. beef stew meat
2 pkgs. onion soup mix
2–10 oz. cans tomato soup
2–10 oz. cans cream of mushroom soup
5 cups water
4 carrots, diced
4 large potatoes, peeled and cubed
3 stalks celery, diced
1 cup frozen green beans
½ t. pepper

Recipe Yield	Prep Time	Total Time
10 servings	20 minutes	4½ hours

Directions

Preheat oven to 350 degrees. In a large Dutch oven, mix stew meat with onion soup mix, tomato soup, cream of mushroom soup, and water. Bake uncovered for 2 hours. Add vegetables and pepper. Stir to combine, then cover and continue baking for 2 more hours, until vegetables are tender.

Ladle into soup bowls and serve with hot French bread, or wow your family or guests by serving in individual bread bowls.

Nutritional Information (per serving): Calories 424.0; Total Fat 16.3g; Cholesterol 64.0mg; Sodium 1300.5mg; Total Carbohydrates 45.1g (Dietary Fiber 5.6g); Protein 5.8g

Honey Glazed Pork Tenderloin

A sweet and tangy Asian marinade makes this tenderloin wonderful!

	x3
⅓ cup honey	1c
2 T. soy sauce	¼c + 2T
1 T. brown sugar	3T
2 T. sesame oil	¼c + 2T
2 T. balsamic vinegar	¼c*
2 (¾ lb. each) pork tenderloins	6 tenderloins (4½ lbs.)

*This measurement has been adjusted to accommodate the intensi-fied flavor of acidic ingredients when recipe is made in quantity.

Recipe Yield

6 servings

Prep Time

10 minutes

Total Time

1 hour 15 minutes

Directions

Preheat oven to 450 degrees. In a medium bowl, mix the honey, soy sauce, brown sugar, sesame oil, and balsamic vinegar together with whisk. Place pork tenderloins in a roasting pan, and roast 15 minutes. Remove pork from oven and baste with honey sauce. Reduce oven temperature to 350 degrees and continue roasting for 45 more minutes, basting tenderloins occasionally.

Freezing Instructions

To make this recipe x3 and freeze the extra meals, use the quantity table listed for the appropriate ingredient amounts. Place tenderloins in freezer bags. Mix remaining ingredients and pour over meat. Freeze, using freezer bag method. On serving day, thaw and roast as directed.

Nutritional Information (per serving): Calories 313.0; Total Fat 11.6g; Cholesterol 89.6mg; Sodium 365.7mg; Total Carbohydrates 17.1g (Dietary Fiber 2.7g); Protein 33.7g

Italian Chicken

Your kids will love this chicken dish!

4 boneless, skinless chicken breasts
1 cup Italian dressing
1¾ cups Ritz crackers, crushed
½ cup freshly grated parmesan cheese
¼ cup unsalted butter
1 T. lemon juice

Recipe Yield

4 servings

Prep Time

15 minutes

Total Time

4 hours 30 minutes

Directions

Place chicken breasts in gallon-sized plastic storage bag. Pour Italian dressing over chicken and marinate in refrigerator for 3–4 hours. Combine cracker crumbs and parmesan cheese. After chicken has marinated, coat each breast with cracker crumb mixture. Place chicken breasts in baking dish and bake uncovered at 350 degrees for 35–45 minutes, until chicken is tender and no longer pink.

While chicken is baking, melt butter in small saucepan and add lemon juice. Simmer for 2–3 minutes. Drizzle lemon butter over chicken and serve immediately.

Nutritional Information (per serving): Calories 754.0; Total Fat 49.9g; Cholesterol 177.8mg; Sodium 951.4mg; Total Carbohydrates 14.3g (Dietary Fiber 0.0g); Protein 45.0g

New Orleans Style Shrimp Packets

*A shrimp dish straight from the South
. . . unique and delicious!*

3 T. Worcestershire sauce
2 T. fresh lemon juice
1 T. butter, melted
2 t. fresh rosemary, chopped
2 t. garlic, chopped
½ t. dried thyme
½ t. hot pepper sauce (such as Tabasco)
¼ t. freshly ground black pepper
¼ t. ground red pepper
2 lbs. large shrimp, peeled
2 lemons, sliced into ¼-inch slices
6 t. (2 T.) butter

Recipe Yield

6 servings

Prep Time

20 minutes

Total Time

50 minutes

Directions

Combine all ingredients except butter in a large bowl; toss well. Cover and marinate in refrigerator for 30 minutes.

Preheat oven to 425 degrees. Fold 6 (16 x 12 inch) sheets of heavy-duty aluminum foil in half crosswise. Open foil. Remove shrimp mixture from bowl; reserve juices. Place about 1½ cups shrimp mixture on half of each foil sheet. Drizzle remaining juices evenly over shrimp. Top each serving of shrimp with 1 t. butter. Fold foil over shrimp; tightly seal edges. Place packets on a baking sheet. Bake for 15 minutes. Let stand 5 minutes. Place on plates. Unfold packets carefully; serve immediately.

Very good with rice and fresh fruit, and this makes a very attractive plate as well!

Nutritional Information (1 packet): Calories 215.0; Total Fat 7.1g; Cholesterol 242.0mg; Sodium 342.0mg; Total Carbohydrates 5.9g (Dietary Fiber 0.53g); Protein 30.9g

One-Dish Dijon Chicken and Roasted Potatoes

Make a side salad and your dinner is complete!

4 boneless, skinless chicken thighs
½ t. salt, divided
½ t. coarsely ground pepper, divided
2 T. Dijon mustard
2 T. honey
1 shallot, minced
½ t. dried thyme
1 lb. new potatoes, halved
olive oil cooking spray

Recipe Yield
4 servings

Prep Time
10 minutes

Total Time
1 hour

Directions

Preheat oven to 350 degrees. Sprinkle chicken thighs with ¼ t. salt and ¼ t. pepper. Place chicken in 9 x 13 baking dish. Mix mustard, honey, shallot, and thyme together in small bowl. Spread over chicken thighs. Add potatoes to baking dish over chicken and spritz with olive oil spray. Sprinkle potatoes with remaining salt and pepper.

Bake uncovered for 50–60 minutes, until chicken is done and potatoes are tender.

Nutritional Information (per serving): Calories 346.0; Total Fat 9.7g; Cholesterol 57.3mg; Sodium 543.4mg; Total Carbohydrates 46.1g (Dietary Fiber 4.8g); Protein 4.8g

Oven Roasted Orange Chicken

This orange dream bakes up crispy golden brown!

1 whole chicken (about 4–5 lbs.)
1 T. kosher salt
1 T. coarsely ground pepper
1 T. garlic salt
1 orange, quartered
1 cup half-and-half, divided
3 T. orange juice or Grand Marnier liqueur

Recipe Yield

6–8 servings

Prep Time

10 minutes

Total Time

2 hours 30 minutes

Directions

Mix together salt, pepper, and garlic salt in a small bowl. Rub salt and pepper mixture over entire chicken, including inside cavities. Place quartered orange inside chicken. Place chicken in a greased roasting pan.

Bake uncovered at 425 degrees for 20 minutes. Reduce oven temperature to 350 degrees. Pour ½ cup of half-and-half over chicken and bake for 20 minutes. Pour remaining half-and-half over chicken and continue to bake for 60–90 minutes, basting every 15 minutes, until chicken is done and juices run clear. Pour orange juice or Grand Marnier over chicken and continue baking for an additional 15 minutes.

Nutritional Information (per serving): Calories 209.0; Total Fat 11.1g; Cholesterol 75.6mg; Sodium 1387.1mg; Total Carbohydrates 5.3g (Dietary Fiber 0.8g); Protein 21.3g

Regal Pork Roast

Sunday roast at its best!

	x3
3 lbs. pork roast	9 lbs
½ cup dry red wine	1½c
½ cup canned cranberry sauce, whole berry	1½c
¼ cup cranberry juice cocktail	¾c
¼ cup honey	¾c
¼ cup apricot preserves	¾c
½ t. dried mustard	1½t
½ t. pepper	1½t

Recipe Yield

8 servings

Prep Time

12 minutes

Total Time

3 ¼ hours

Directions

Place roast in a 2-quart baking dish. Mix remaining ingredients and pour over roast. Bake, covered, at 350 degrees for 2½–3 hours, until meat thermometer registers 160–165 degrees. Bake uncovered for last 30 minutes of baking time to brown roast.

Freezing Instructions

To make this recipe x3 and freeze the extra meals, use the quantity table listed for the appropriate ingredient amounts. Place uncooked roasts in freezer bags. Mix remaining ingredients and pour over meat. Freeze, using freezer bag method. On serving day, thaw and roast as directed.

Nutritional Information (per serving): Calories 637.0; Total Fat 40.8g; Cholesterol 159.8mg; Sodium 128.8mg; Total Carbohydrates 23.3g (Dietary Fiber 0.2g); Protein 40.0g

Rosemary Chicken with Shallots and Sweet Potatoes

*An easy and elegant dish, great
for a weeknight family meal and guests alike!*

Sweet Potatoes

1½ lbs. sweet potatoes or yams, peeled and cut into 2-inch pieces
1 t. kosher salt
2 T. butter
2 T. brown sugar

Chicken

¼ cup olive oil, divided
4 boneless, skinless chicken breasts
1 t. kosher salt, divided
½ t. pepper, divided
4 shallots, sliced into thin rings
1 T. fresh rosemary, roughly chopped

Recipe Yield	**Prep Time**	**Total Time**
4 servings	30 minutes	30 minutes

Directions

Place sweet potatoes or yams in a large pot. Add just enough cold water to cover and bring water to a boil. Add 1 t. salt and reduce heat to a simmer. Simmer potatoes for 15 minutes or until tender. Reserve ¼ cup of the cooking water and drain the sweet potatoes. Return potatoes to the pot and coarsely mash with reserved cooking water, butter, and brown sugar.

While potatoes are boiling, heat 1 T. of the oil in a large skillet over medium-high heat. Season chicken breasts with ½ t. salt and ¼ t. pepper and cook until golden brown and cooked through, approximately 7–8 minutes per side. Transfer chicken to a large serving plate.

Wipe out the skillet and use to heat remaining 3 T. of oil over medium-high heat. Add shallots, rosemary, ½ t. salt, and ¼ t. pepper and cook, stirring, until shallots are tender, 3–4 minutes. Drizzle shallot mixture over chicken, and place mashed sweet potatoes alongside chicken on the serving plate.

Nutritional Information (per serving): Calories 478.2; Total Fat 9.4g; Cholesterol 144.0mg; Sodium 226.7mg; Total Carbohydrates 41.8g (Dietary Fiber 4.5g); Protein 56.7g

Sesame Chicken with Hoisin Dipping Sauce

The spicy Asian sauce is what sets this dish apart.

2 lbs. boneless, skinless chicken thighs

⅓ cup (approx. 4 oz.) hoisin sauce*

2 T. sesame seeds (white and/or black)

Dipping Sauce

2 T. sweet chili sauce

1½ t. fresh ginger, peeled and chopped

1½ t. rice vinegar

¼ t. Chinese five-spice powder**

*Hoisin sauce is found in the ethnic food aisle of most grocery stores. Any remaining sauce can be stored in the refrigerator.

**Chinese five-spice powder is found in the spices/seasoning section of the grocery store.

Recipe Yield	Prep Time	Total Time
4–6 servings	15 minutes	30 minutes

Directions

Preheat oven to 400 degrees. Place chicken thighs in a jelly roll pan or shallow baking pan. Baste one side of chicken with hoisin sauce and sprinkle lightly with sesame seeds, then turn chicken over and repeat for other side. Reserve remaining hoisin sauce. Bake thighs for 20–25 minutes until juices run clear.

While chicken is baking, prepare the dipping sauce in a microwave-safe bowl, mixing together the sauce ingredients and reserved hoisin sauce. Set aside.

Just before chicken is done baking, heat the dipping sauce in microwave for 40–45 seconds, stirring once. Serve with chicken. This sauce stores well and can be reheated as needed.

Nutritional Information (per serving): Calories 263.9; Total Fat 8.8g; Cholesterol 143.7mg; Sodium 482.1mg; Total Carbohydrates 9.4g (Dietary Fiber 0.8g); Protein 35.0g

Shirley's Mini Meatloaves

A Midwest favorite for any size family!

Contributed by Shirley Burke—Westminster, Colorado

	x3
Meatloaf	
2 lbs. ground beef	6 lbs
½ cup onion, chopped	1½c
¼ cup green pepper, chopped	¾c
¼ cup celery, chopped	¾c
½ t. salt	1½t
¼ t. black pepper	¾t
½ t. dried parsley	1½t
½ t. dried basil	1½t
½ cup saltine cracker crumbs	1½c
¼ cup ketchup	¾c
2 eggs	6
¼ cup milk	¾c
Glaze	
¼ cup ketchup	
1 T. brown sugar	

Recipe Yield	**Prep Time**	**Total Time**
16 servings	15 minutes	1 hour 15 minutes

Directions

For meatloaf: in a large mixing bowl, mix all meatloaf ingredients with a large spoon until well blended. Shape mixture into 4 mini-loaves. Arrange loaves in a 9 x 13 casserole dish, keeping edges of meatloaves from touching each other. Meatloaves may also be placed in individual mini-loaf pans for baking.

For glaze: mix together ketchup and brown sugar. Brush glaze on top of each loaf. Bake uncovered in 350 degree oven for about 1 hour.

Freezing Instructions

To make this recipe x3 and freeze the extra meatloaves, use the quantity table listed for the appropriate ingredient amounts. Wrap each raw meatloaf in plastic wrap, then place in a freezer bag. Freeze, using freezer bag method. On serving day, thaw, add glaze, and bake as directed.

Nutritional Information (per serving): Calories 126.0; Total Fat 5.2g; Cholesterol 63.2mg; Sodium 214.2 mg; Total Carbohydrates 6.3g (Dietary Fiber 0.3g); Protein 13.5g

Tender Baked Meatballs

Tasty morsels—for meatball sandwiches or pasta and sauce!

1 small onion, finely diced
⅔ cup parmesan cheese, grated
⅓ cup breadcrumbs
1 large egg, beaten
½ cup fresh Italian flat leaf parsley, chopped (or ¼ cup, dried)
2 medium cloves garlic, minced
2 T. ketchup
¾ t. kosher salt
½ t. pepper
pinch of red pepper flakes or cayenne pepper
1 lb. ground beef or bison (or combination of ½ lb. beef and ½ lb. Italian sausage)

Recipe Yield

6 servings (approximately 16 meatballs)

Prep Time

15 minutes

Total Time

30 minutes

Directions

Preheat oven to 400 degrees, positioning oven rack in lower third of oven. Line a baking sheet with parchment paper or foil.

In a large mixing bowl, combine all ingredients except meat. Briefly stir to mix ingredients together. Add the beef, using your hands, and gently combine all the ingredients together just until incorporated, being careful not to overwork the meat (see tip).

Pinch off about 1 ½-inch pieces of meat mixture and gently form into meatballs, placing

Tip

For a quick cleanup and no messy hands, wear disposable latex gloves when you mix with your hands.

on prepared baking sheet. Bake meatballs for about 15 minutes until just cooked through. (If meatballs are to be simmered in sauce, slightly under bake, as they will continue to bake in sauce.)

Nutritional Information (per serving): Calories 358.7; Total Fat 24.9g; Cholesterol 108.4mg; Sodium 694.4mg; Total Carbohydrates 12.5g (Dietary Fiber 1.0g); Protein 20.1g

Grate Grills and Marinades

Apricot Glazed Salmon

This sweet glaze enhances the flavor of the salmon.

1½ lbs. salmon fillets
⅓ cup olive oil
½ t. kosher salt
½ t. pepper

Glaze

3 T. unsalted butter
1 cup (8 oz.) apricot preserves
2 T. Dijon mustard
1 T. + 2 t. soy sauce
¼ t. cayenne pepper (optional)

½ cup slivered or sliced almonds, toasted (for topping)

Recipe Yield	**Prep Time**	**Total Time**
6 servings	15 minutes	30 minutes

Directions

Preheat grill to medium heat. Baste salmon with olive oil; sprinkle with salt and pepper. Mix glaze ingredients together in a small bowl. Grill salmon over medium heat, basting several times with glaze, until salmon is done and flakes when tested with fork. Serve with toasted almonds sprinkled on top.

Nutritional Information (per serving): Calories 486.9; Total Fat 30.9g; Cholesterol 95.7mg; Sodium 406.9mg; Total Carbohydrates 20.1g (Dietary Fiber 1.3g); Protein 30.7g

BBQ Espresso Spareribs

Fall-off-the-bone good!

Sauce

1 T. vegetable oil
1 cup onion, chopped
2 cloves garlic, minced
2–3 small jalapeño peppers, seeded and finely chopped (optional, to taste)
½ cup brown sugar, packed
½ cup red wine vinegar
½ cup espresso or strong coffee
½ cup beef or chicken stock
2 T. Worcestershire sauce
2 T. molasses
½ T. ground cumin
½ t. cinnamon
½ T. regular or ancho chile powder
1 t. salt
½ t. ground pepper
1¼ cup ketchup

Ribs

2 racks spare ribs (beef or pork)
salt and pepper

Recipe Yield	**Prep Time**	**Total Time**
6 servings	20 minutes	2 hours 30 minutes

Directions

For the sauce: Heat oil in saucepan over medium-high heat. Add onions, garlic, and jalapeños, and sauté until onions are tender, about 6 minutes. Add remaining sauce ingredients to pan, stirring to incorporate. Simmer over low heat for 15–20 minutes. For a smoother sauce, pour into blender or food processor and puree. The sauce can be made ahead and stored for up to 1 week in the refrigerator until ready to use.

For the ribs: preheat oven to 325 degrees. Cut each rack of ribs in thirds along the bone so they can be easily handled. Sprinkle liberally with salt and pepper on both sides and pat into the meat. Place ribs on a rimmed baking sheet lined with parchment paper or foil for easy cleanup. They may overlap. Place ribs in the oven and bake until they are tender and almost falling off the bone, about 2 hours. Rotate the layers of ribs every 30 minutes if they have been stacked to fit onto the baking sheet. (Ribs may also be prepared in the crockpot, following your crockpot manufacturer guidelines.)

Transfer ribs to grill preheated on low heat. Brush ribs with sauce and grill for about 30 minutes, basting and turning every 10 minutes, until the ribs are well glazed.

Nutritional Information (per serving): Calories 462.8; Total Fat 31.0g; Cholesterol 86.1mg; Sodium 1346.6mg; Total Carbohydrates 25.3g (Dietary Fiber 0.2g); Protein 19.0g

Beef and Pineapple Skewers

A wonderful, unique marinade and dipping sauce.

Sauce

2 cups fresh parsley
½ cup fresh mint leaves
¼ cup fresh cilantro
1 clove garlic
2 T. red wine vinegar
1 t. crushed chili flakes (or ¼ t. cayenne pepper)
1 t. sugar
1½ t. salt
½ t. pepper
½ cup olive oil

Beef

1½ lbs. beef fillet or sirloin, cut into ¾-inch cubes (about 40 cubes)
1 lb. fresh pineapple, cut into ¾-inch pieces (or 1½ cups canned pineapple chunks)
20–8-inch wooden or bamboo skewers, soaked in water for 30 minutes
salt and freshly ground pepper

Recipe Yield	**Prep Time**	**Total Time**
20 skewers	25 minutes	2 hours 30 minutes

Directions

For the sauce: in a blender or food processor, blend all sauce ingredients except oil until smooth. With the machine running, gradually add the olive oil until incorporated. Place half of the sauce in a small serving bowl, then cover with plastic wrap and refrigerate until ready to serve.

For the skewers: place beef in medium bowl with remaining half of sauce. Toss until beef is coated with sauce. Cover and refrigerate for 3 hours.

Preheat grill to medium-high, or place a grill pan on stove over medium-high heat. Thread beef on skewers, alternating with pieces of pineapple. Grill the skewers for 2–3 minutes each side (for medium rare) or until desired doneness. Season with salt and pepper.

To serve, arrange skewers on a serving platter. Drizzle with remaining reserved sauce or serve the sauce on the side as a condiment.

Nutritional Information (per serving): Calories 281.6; Total Fat 18.6g; Cholesterol 61.0mg, Sodium 329.3mg; Total Carbohydrates 7.5g (Dietary Fiber 1.0g); Protein 21.3g

Beef Kabobs with Peanut Lime Dipping Sauce

The peanut lime dipping sauce makes these kabobs outrageously good!

	x3
1½ lbs. top sirloin	4½ lbs
Marinade	
¼ cup water	¾c
⅓ cup ketchup	1c
¼ cup soy sauce	¾c
3 T. brown sugar	½c + 1T
3 T. lime juice	½c*
1 T. peanut oil	3T
½ t. ginger	1½t
1 t. garlic, minced	1T
¼ t. red pepper flakes	¾t
Serving Day	
¼ cup creamy peanut butter	
6 wooden skewers	

*This measurement has been adjusted to accommodate the intensified flavor of acidic ingredients when recipe is made in quantity.

Recipe Yield	**Prep Time**	**Total Time**
4–6 servings	30 minutes	2 hours 30 minutes

Directions

Cut sirloin into ¾-inch cubes, then place in freezer bag. Whisk together marinade ingredients and pour over meat. Place in refrigerator and marinate for 2 hours. Remove meat from bag, reserving marinade. Thread meat onto skewers, leaving space between the meat pieces. Grill over direct medium heat to desired doneness.

Pour reserved marinade into small saucepan. Bring to a full boil over high heat, and continue boiling for an additional minute. Reduce heat to medium. Add peanut butter, then return sauce to boiling, stirring constantly, and continue cooking until peanut butter is well blended and sauce is thickened. Remove meat from skewers and serve with dipping sauce.

Freezing Instructions

To make this recipe x3 and freeze the extra meals, use the quantity table listed for the appropriate ingredient amounts. Place meat in freezer bags. Mix marinade ingredients and pour over meat. Freeze, using freezer bag method. On serving day, thaw and cook as directed.

Nutritional Information (per serving): Calories 363.0; Total Fat 16.8g; Cholesterol 100.9mg; Sodium 843.7mg; Total Carbohydrates 16.9g (Dietary Fiber 0.8g); Protein 37.8g

Best Ever Marinated Chicken

A delicious grilled chicken for a summer barbecue.

	x3
3 lbs. boneless chicken breasts	9 lbs
⅓ cup soy sauce	1c
2 T. lemon juice	¼c*
¼ t. onion power	¾t
¼ t. garlic powder	¾t
¼ t. poultry seasoning	¾t
1 T. dried parsley flakes	3T

*This measurement has been adjusted to accommodate the intensified flavor of acidic ingredients when recipe is made in quantity.

Recipe Yield

6 servings

Prep Time

10 minutes

Total Time

4 hours 30 minutes

Directions

Place chicken breasts in a large baking dish. Combine remaining ingredients and pour over chicken, cover, and marinate in refrigerator for 4–6 hours. Grill over medium heat, turning once, until chicken is tender and juices run clear.

Freezing Instructions

To make this recipe x3 and freeze the extra meals, use the quantity table listed for the appropriate ingredient amounts. Place chicken in freezer bags. Mix remaining ingredients and pour over chicken. Freeze, using freezer bag method. On serving day, thaw and cook as directed.

Nutritional Information (per serving): Calories 209.0; Total Fat 1.0g; Cholesterol 110.0mg; Sodium 1251.6mg; Total Carbohydrates 1.6g (Dietary Fiber 0.2g); Protein 46.9g

Buffalo Chicken Burgers with Bleu Cheese Sauce

Sets your taste buds on fire!

Bleu Cheese Sauce

¼ cup reduced-fat sour cream

2 oz. bleu cheese, crumbled

¼ cup light mayonnaise

2 t. cider vinegar

½ t. Worcestershire sauce

Burgers

1¼ lbs. ground chicken (or turkey)

1 large stalk celery, finely chopped

¼ cup onion, finely minced

3 T. hot pepper sauce (such as hot wings sauce)

Buffalo Sauce

½ cup hot pepper sauce

2 T. butter, melted

4 hamburger buns

lettuce leaves

carrot and celery sticks

Recipe Yield	**Prep Time**	**Total Time**
4 servings	20 minutes	35 minutes

Directions

To make bleu cheese sauce: in small bowl, stir together sauce ingredients until blended. Set aside. Makes about ¾ cup.

To make burgers: in medium bowl, combine chicken, celery, onion, and hot pepper sauce, stirring just until mixture is incorporated, being careful not to overmix. Shape mixture into four ¾-inch-thick burgers. Spray both sides of burgers with nonstick cooking spray.

To make buffalo sauce: in a small bowl, heat hot sauce and melted butter in microwave for 30–60 seconds; stir.

Preheat grill to medium, or preheat a grill pan on stove over medium heat. Grill burgers, turning once, until meat loses its pink color throughout, about 12–14 minutes. Burgers should reach an internal temperature of 165 degrees. Quickly dip cooked burgers in the hot buffalo sauce before placing on buns.

Serve burgers on buns with lettuce and a dollop of bleu cheese sauce. Serve remaining sauce with carrot and celery sticks. Pass around additional hot pepper sauce if you like.

Nutritional Information for Burgers (per serving): Calories 373.8; Total Fat 25.8g; Cholesterol 140.5mg; Sodium 906.0 mg; Total Carbohydrates 4.3g (Dietary Fiber 0.3g); Protein 29.9g.

Nutritional Information for Bleu Cheese Sauce (per serving): Calories 131.0; Total Fat 12.0g; Cholesterol 22.2mg; Sodium 330.5mg; Total Carbohydrates 2.4g (Dietary Fiber 0.0g); Protein 3.6g

Tip

For a quick cleanup and no messy hands, wear disposable latex gloves when you mix with your hands.

Cajun Mahi Mahi

Serve as a main dish for dinner
or as a blackened fish sandwich for lunch!

4 Mahi Mahi fillets (1½ lbs.)

Cajun Seasoning

1 T. paprika

2½ T. salt

1 T. onion powder

1 T. garlic powder

1 T. cayenne pepper

¾ T. white pepper

¾ T. black pepper

1½ t. thyme

1½ t. oregano

¾ t. sage

Recipe Yield	**Prep Time**	**Total Time**
4 servings	20 minutes	20 minutes

Directions

Combine all Cajun seasoning ingredients in small bowl; set aside. Rinse fillets and pat dry. Sprinkle each side of fillets with Cajun seasoning. Place fillets on a greased grill, preheated to medium-high, arranging so they do not touch each other. Grill 4–5 minutes per side, or until fish flakes easily.

Nutritional Information (per serving): Calories 203.0; Total Fat 2.2g; Cholesterol 160.0mg; Sodium 780.0mg; Total Carbohydrates 5.3g (Dietary Fiber 1.5g); Protein 40.9g

Cedar Plank Grilled Salmon with Garlic, Lemon, and Dill

Can also be placed directly on the grill without a plank.

A creation of Jack Sunahara—Castle Rock, Colorado

---

1 cedar plank for grilling

3 lbs. salmon

Marinade

6 T. extra virgin olive oil

4 large garlic cloves, minced

¼ cup fresh dill, minced

2 t. salt

1 t. pepper

1 t. lemon zest

½ t. lemon juice

1 T. soy sauce

3 T. chardonnay

½ t. ground ginger

1 T. brown sugar

lemon juice for serving

Recipe Yield	**Prep Time**	**Total Time**
8 servings	30 minutes	45 minutes

Directions

Soak cedar plank in water overnight.

Heat grill on high for 10 minutes. Meanwhile, combine all marinade ingredients in a bowl. Place salmon in marinade, turning to coat. Marinate at room temperature for 20 minutes.

Place soaked cedar plank on hot grill; close lid and allow plank to sit until it starts to smoke, about 5 minutes. Transfer salmon to hot plank, turn grill to low, and cook until salmon is just opaque throughout, about 20–25 minutes, depending on plank thickness and grill temperature. Remove from grill and sprinkle with lemon juice.

Serve with fresh garden salad and rice.

Nutritional Information (per serving): Calories 357.0; Total Fat 17.7g; Cholesterol 113.9mg; Sodium 663.0mg; Total Carbohydrates 3.3g (Dietary Fiber 0.0g); Protein 43.7g

Chicken, Beef, Shrimp, and Mushroom Skewers for the Grill

A wonderful assortment of flavors—your guests won't know which one to try next!

	x3
Skewer Items	
1½ lbs. sirloin or flat iron steak, cut into 1-inch thick strips	4½ lbs
2 boneless, skinless chicken breasts, cut into 1-inch thick strips	6
1¼ lbs. medium shrimp in shell, peeled and deveined	3¾ lbs
1 lb. mushrooms, halved if stems are large	
Marinade	
6 large cloves of garlic	18
2½ t. salt	2T + 1½t
2 T. fresh lemon juice	¼c +2T
½ t. black pepper	1½t
⅓ cup olive oil	1c
70 small or 35 large wooden skewers, soaked in water for 30 min.	

Recipe Yield

70 appetizer skewers (25 servings) or 35 entree skewers (15 servings)

Prep Time

30 minutes

Total Time

1 hour 15 minutes

Directions

Mince garlic and mash into a paste with the salt, using a large, heavy knife. Transfer to a small bowl and whisk in lemon juice and pepper. Whisk in olive oil and mix well. Divide marinade into 4 bowls or freezer bags.

Add beef to the first bag, chicken to the second bag, shrimp to the third bag, and mushrooms to the final bag. Marinate in refrigerator for 45 minutes. Remove from bags and thread onto skewers.

Preheat grill on high heat. Cook beef and chicken skewers to desired doneness, approximately 3–5 minutes per side. Cook shrimp until just done, approximately 2 minutes per side. Cook mushrooms until tender, approximately 3 minutes.

Freezing Instructions

To make this recipe x3 and freeze the extra meals, use the quantity table listed for the appropriate ingredient amounts. Place beef, chicken, and shrimp in 3 different freezer bags. Mix marinade ingredients, divide, and add to each bag. Freeze, using freezer bag method. On serving day, thaw and grill as directed. Note: mushrooms should be grilled fresh and not frozen.

Nutritional Information (per meat appetizer skewer): Calories 55.0; Total Fat 2.6g; Cholesterol 41.6mg; Sodium 113.0mg; Total Carbohydrates 0.3g (Dietary Fiber 0.1g); Protein 7.3g

Chipotle Peanut Barbecue Chicken

A unique combination of southwestern and Asian flavors.

6–8 boneless, skinless chicken thighs
1 t. lemon pepper seasoning
1 t. kosher salt

Sauce

1 cup barbecue sauce
⅓ cup creamy peanut butter
⅓ cup orange juice
¼ cup honey
1 T. chipotle pepper in adobo sauce, drained and chopped*

*Canned chipotle pepper in adobo sauce is found in the Mexican ingredient section of the grocery store.

Recipe Yield	**Prep Time**	**Total Time**
6–8 servings	30 minutes	30 minutes

Directions

Preheat grill to medium heat. Sprinkle chicken with lemon pepper seasoning and kosher salt. Set aside.

In a small saucepan, combine sauce ingredients and cook over medium-low heat, until well combined and heated through, about 3 minutes. Do not boil.

Grill chicken thighs over medium heat, turning once, until chicken is tender and no longer pink, approximately 15–20 minutes. Brush one side of chicken with chipotle peanut sauce and grill an additional 3–5 minutes. Flip chicken and repeat. Remove from grill and serve with remaining warm chipotle peanut sauce on the side.

Nutritional Information (per serving): Calories 206.0; Total Fat 8.7g; Cholesterol 57.3mg; Sodium 654.0mg; Total Carbohydrates 15.9g (Dietary Fiber 1.1g); Protein 16.9g

Classic Beer Can Chicken

*A unique idea that results in moist
and delicious roasted chicken every time!*

1 whole roasting chicken (4–5 lbs.)
2 T. olive oil
3 T. dry spice rub, divided (optional)
1 t. kosher salt
½ t. freshly ground black pepper
1–12 oz. can of beer (may use nonalcoholic beer if desired)

Recipe Yield	**Prep Time**	**Total Time**
6 servings	15 minutes	1 hour 30 minutes

Directions

Preheat grill to medium heat. Remove neck and giblets from roasting chicken, rinse, and pat dry with paper towels. Brush chicken all over with oil and season with 2 T. spice rub or simply with salt and pepper. Set aside.

Open beer can, pour out about ¼ cup of the beer, and punch an extra hole in top of the can with can opener. Sprinkle the remaining 1 T. spice rub inside beer can, if using.

Hold chicken above beer can and slide chicken over the can, making sure the legs are in front of the can. Fold the wings back behind the chicken.

Place chicken in the center of the grill's cooking grate, keeping beer can upright. The chicken will appear to be "sitting" or resting on the grate. (There are also vertical roasting racks sold at cooking stores for this very purpose, if you choose to invest in one.)

Cook chicken for approximately one hour, or until the internal temperature registers 165 degrees in the breast area. Remove from grill and let rest for 10 minutes before removing beer can and carving.

Nutritional Information (per serving): Calories 105.6; Total Fat 6.1g; Cholesterol 29.3mg; Sodium 20.8mg; Total Carbohydrates 0.4g (Dietary Fiber 0.0g); Protein 10.6g

Grilled Carne Asada

A delicious, classic Mexican meal.

	x3
2 lbs. flank steak	6 lbs
Marinade	
¼ cup paprika	¾c
¼ cup chili powder	¾c
1 cup cilantro, chopped	3c
1 garlic clove, minced	3
2 t. dried oregano	2T
1 T. salt	3T
1 T. pepper	3T
¼ cup lime juice	½c*
¼ cup extra virgin olive oil	¾c
Serving Day	
8 corn or flour tortillas	
tomatoes, chopped	
avocado slices	

*This measurement has been adjusted to accommodate the intensified flavor of acidic ingredients when recipe is made in quantity.

Recipe Yield

8 servings

Prep Time

25 minutes

Total Time

4 hours 30 minutes

Directions

Place steak in a glass baking dish. Combine marinade ingredients in a food processor or blender and blend until smooth. Spoon a layer of marinade over both sides of meat. Cover and marinate in refrigerator for 4–24 hours.

Remove steak from baking dish and grill over medium heat to desired doneness. Slice thin. Serve with warm corn or flour tortillas, tomatoes, and avocado slices.

Freezing Instructions

To make this recipe x3 and freeze the extra meals, use the quantity table listed for the appropriate ingredient amounts. Place flank steaks in freezer bags. Mix marinade as directed above and pour over meat. Freeze, using freezer bag method. On serving day, thaw and grill as directed.

Nutritional Information (per serving): Calories 326.0; Total Fat 18.7g; Cholesterol 48.8mg; Sodium 135.7mg; Total Carbohydrates 41.1g (Dietary Fiber 0.8g); Protein 3.1g

Hint

For a freshly roasted taste, place tortillas on upper rack of grill and lightly toast just before serving. Assemble into soft tacos and enjoy!

Grilled Flat Iron Steak Sandwiches

*A mouthwatering steak sandwich
with two different tasty toppers.*

Rub

2 T. brown sugar, packed
2 T. chili powder
2 T. cumin
¼ t. cayenne pepper (or more to taste)
2 t. garlic, minced
2 t. cider vinegar
1 t. Worcestershire sauce

1½ lbs. flat iron steaks
6 baguettes or steak rolls for sandwiches, split

Recipe Yield	**Prep Time**	**Total Time**
6 servings	20 minutes for steak, 10 minutes for topping	45 minutes

Directions

To make steak rub: combine all ingredients into a small bowl, mixing thoroughly. Press rub evenly onto both sides of steak. Let stand 10 minutes to marinate. (This can also be done ahead, wrapping steak in plastic wrap and refrigerating until ready to grill.) While meat is marinating, prepare one of the topping recipes below.

Heat grill to medium heat. When grill is hot, spray steak with cooking spray and grill to desired doneness, about 10–14 minutes, turning occasionally to avoid burning. Let steak rest for 5–10 minutes, lightly covered with foil to keep warm. Slice steak across the grain into thin slices. Place steak slices on rolls or baguettes and add one of your prepared toppers. Serve.

Toppers

Bleu cheese, mushroom, and caramelized onion

1 medium onion, red or yellow, chopped
1–2 T. olive oil
⅛ t. salt, or more to taste
1–8 oz. package sliced mushrooms
bleu cheese crumbles

While meat is marinating, in a large skillet sauté onion in 1 T. olive oil over medium heat for about 5–7 minutes. Sprinkle salt over onions. Stir in sliced mushrooms, adding more oil if necessary. Continue sautéing until mushrooms are cooked, about 3–5 minutes. Layer the onion/mushroom mixture on top of steak slices, followed by a sprinkling of bleu cheese.

Queso fresca, salsa, and avocado

1 medium onion, red or yellow, chopped
1 T. olive oil
⅛ t. salt, or more to taste
pinch cayenne pepper, or 1 t. fresh jalapeño pepper, finely diced (more or less to taste)
1 large tomato, diced
1 avocado, sliced
¼ cup Monterey jack cheese, shredded
lime wedges (optional)

While meat is marinating, in a large skillet sauté onion in 1 T. olive oil over medium heat for about 5–7 minutes. Sprinkle salt over onions. Add jalapeños (or cayenne pepper) and tomato to onion, just until heated through. (If you prefer uncooked tomatoes, mix the fresh, diced tomatoes and jalapeño together in a small side bowl.) Layer sliced meat on rolls, followed by onion and tomato mixture. Top with avocado slices followed by a sprinkling of cheese. Finish with a squeeze of fresh lime juice, if desired.

Nutritional Information (per serving, without topper): Calories 286.1; Total Fat 15.4g; Cholesterol 94.1mg; Sodium 117.9mg; Total Carbohydrates 8.8g (Dietary Fiber 1.1g); Protein 29.0g

Grilled Rib Eye Steaks with Java Rub

The espresso beans in the rub make this recipe unique!

	x3
4–8oz. rib eye steaks, bone in	12
Rub	
¼ cup finely ground espresso beans	¾c
2 T. ancho chili powder	¼c + 2T
4 t. brown sugar	¼c
1 t. kosher salt	1T
1 t. dried basil	1T
1 t. coriander	1T
1 t. dry mustard	1T
olive oil spray	

Recipe Yield	**Prep Time**	**Total Time**
4 servings	15 minutes	35–45 minutes

Directions

For rub, mix dry ingredients together in a small bowl. Spritz each side of steaks with olive oil spray. Sprinkle rub onto each side of steaks. Let steaks sit at room temperature for 30 minutes. Grill over medium direct heat to desired doneness.

Freezing Instructions

To make this recipe x3 and freeze the extra steaks, use the quantity table listed for the appropriate ingredient amounts. After spritzing each steak with olive oil, place rub on each side of steak, then wrap each steak individually in plastic wrap. Place wrapped steaks in freezer bag. Freeze, using freezer bag method. On serving day, thaw and grill as directed.

Nutritional Information (per serving): Calories 390.0; Total Fat 17.8g; Cholesterol 88.5mg; Sodium 752.8mg; Total Carbohydrates 8.5g (Dietary Fiber 1.5g); Protein 48.9g

Luscious Grilled Pork Tenderloin

The combination of marinade and rub gives this tenderloin great flavor!

	x3
2 pork tenderloins, 1 lb. each	6
Marinade	
⅓ cup orange juice	1c
2 T. olive oil	¼c + 2T
2 T. Worcestershire sauce	¼c + 2T
1 T. molasses	3T
1 t. garlic, minced	1T
Rub	
1 t. chili powder	1T
1 t. coarsely ground pepper	1T
1 t. kosher salt	1T
½ t. cumin	1½t
½ t. dried oregano	1½t
¼ t. garlic powder	¾t

Recipe Yield

8 servings

Prep Time

20 minutes

Total Time

3 hours 30 minutes

Directions

In a small bowl, mix together marinade ingredients. Place tenderloins in freezer bag, then pour marinade over meat. Marinate in refrigerator for 2 hours. Remove tenderloins from refrigerator and place on a large platter. In a small bowl, mix together the dry ingredients for rub, then sprinkle on each side of tenderloins, rubbing spices into the meat. Let sit at room temperature for 30 minutes.

Grill over medium heat for 30–45 minutes, turning once. Internal meat temperature should be 155 degrees, and center of tenderloin should be barely pink. Remove meat from grill, cover with foil, and allow to rest for 10 minutes prior to slicing.

Freezing Instructions

To make this recipe x3 and freeze the extra meals, use the quantity table listed for the appropriate ingredient amounts. Place tenderloin in freezer bags. Mix marinade ingredients and pour over meat. Freeze, using freezer bag method. On serving day, thaw and apply rub to tenderloin, then follow directions for grilling.

Nutritional Information (per serving): Calories 278.0; Total Fat 13.0g; Cholesterol 89.6mg; Sodium 404.2mg; Total Carbohydrates 4.2g (Dietary Fiber 2.9g); Protein 33.6g

Rib Eye Steaks with Parsley-Garlic Butter

An easy jazz-up for your rib eyes—exquisite taste.

Steak

3–1½-inch thick rib eye steaks (about 1 lb. each)
salt and pepper

Parsley-Garlic Butter

½ cup butter (1 stick), softened
1 T. fresh parsley, finely chopped
1 T. fresh chives, chopped
1 clove garlic, pressed
2 t. white cooking wine
¼ t. salt
⅛ t. pepper

Recipe Yield	**Prep Time**	**Total Time**
6 servings	20 minutes	30 minutes

Directions

Mix together all parsley-garlic butter ingredients in a small bowl. Cover and chill.

Heat grill to medium-high heat. Rub steaks with generous amount of salt and pepper. Grill steaks to desired doneness, about 5 minutes per side for medium-rare. Let rest for 5–10 minutes. Cut each steak in half and top with a spoonful of parsley-garlic butter just prior to serving.

Nutritional Information (per serving): Calories 406.0; Total Fat 26.0g; Cholesterol 118.0mg; Sodium 230.0mg; Total Carbohydrates 0.3g (Dietary Fiber 0.1g); Protein 40.0g

Steakhouse Burritos

Wrap up your steak with your Caesar salad and enjoy!

1 lb. boneless top sirloin steak
salt and pepper to taste

Filling Ingredients

4 strips bacon, diced and sautéed
2 cups romaine lettuce, shredded
1 cup cherry tomatoes, halved
½ cup bleu cheese crumbles
¼ cup Caesar dressing

4–12-inch flour tortillas

Recipe Yield	**Prep Time**	**Total Time**
4 servings	25 minutes	25 minutes

Directions

To make filling: combine cooked bacon, romaine, tomatoes, and bleu cheese in a large bowl. Toss with Caesar dressing and chill until ready to use.

Preheat grill to high. Season steak with salt and pepper. Grill 8 minutes for medium-rare, turning once. Remove from heat, tent with foil, and let rest for 5 minutes. While steak rests, heat tortillas until warmed through. Slice steak into thin strips across the grain. Divide steak evenly between 4 tortillas, arranging down the center of each tortilla. Top with ½ cup salad mixture, then roll tortillas to form burritos and cut in half diagonally.

Nutritional Information (per serving): Calories 590.0; Total Fat 25.0g; Cholesterol 120.0mg; Sodium 577.0mg; Total Carbohydrates 29.0g (Dietary Fiber 2.0g); Protein 47.6g

Tahitian Chicken

A tangy taste of the tropics for your next get-together.

Sauce

¼ cup rice wine vinegar

2 cups (16 oz.) pineapple juice

2½ T. hoisin sauce

2 T. ketchup

2 t. soy sauce

2 T. brown sugar

1 T. freshly grated ginger root

2–3 medium cloves garlic, minced

2 T. cornstarch

6 boneless, skinless chicken breasts

2–3 whole green onions, thinly sliced, divided

Recipe Yield	**Prep Time**	**Total Time**
6 servings	15 minutes	40–60 minutes

Directions

In a medium saucepan, whisk sauce ingredients together over medium-low heat until bubbling and beginning to thicken. Remove from heat and cool.

Place chicken pieces in a 9 x 13 baking pan. Sprinkle ⅓ of the sliced green onions over chicken. Divide the sauce, reserving ⅔ for serving. Pour remaining ⅓ of sauce over chicken. Turn chicken pieces in sauce to coat. Allow chicken to marinate for 20–30 minutes in refrigerator.

Grill chicken over a medium-hot grill 30–40 minutes, or until done. Do not overcook. Allow chicken to rest a few minutes before slicing. Slice chicken breasts and top with reserved sauce and a sprinkling of remaining green onions. Serve with a side of rice.

Nutritional Information (per serving): Calories 363.9; Total Fat 3.2g; Cholesterol 137.1mg; Sodium 765.7mg; Total Carbohydrates 25.8g (Dietary Fiber 0.9g); Protein 55.1g

Savory Skillets and Quick Sautés

Basic Beef Mix

Prepare this recipe, divide and freeze, and you're ready to make several different dinners: sloppy joes, tacos, and spaghetti sauce.

4 lbs. ground beef
2 large onions, finely chopped
2–3 cloves garlic, minced (or 1 T. garlic salt)
salt and freshly ground pepper, to taste

Recipe Yield	**Prep Time**	**Total Time**
16 total servings	20 minutes	45 minutes

Directions

Basic beef mix: in a large nonstick skillet or deep saucepan, cook beef, onion, and garlic over medium heat until beef is brown and crumbly, stirring occasionally. Drain and discard fat. Return to pan. Continue with option one or two.

Option One (for Tacos, Nachos, Enchiladas, or Burritos)

Add 1–1½ cups diced green chiles, 1½ cups water, and 2 cups salsa (your choice) to meat in skillet. Cover and simmer over medium-low heat, stirring occasionally, for 15–20 minutes or until liquid is absorbed. If needed, season with additional salt and pepper to taste.

Option Two (for Spaghetti or Sloppy Joes)

Add 4–15 oz. cans diced or crushed tomatoes, 3 t. dried basil or Italian seasoning, 3 T. tomato paste, and 1 cup chopped green pepper (optional) to skillet. Cover and simmer over medium-low heat, stirring occasionally, for 15–20 minutes or until mixture is cooked through. If needed, add additional salt, pepper, or seasonings to taste. (For spaghetti sauce, 1½–2 cups grated parmesan or Romano cheese can be added. For sloppy joes, 2 T. of brown sugar can be added, if you like a sweeter mixture.)

For All Mixes

Cool meat mixture before dividing into 4–1 lb. portions. Refrigerate or freeze for future use. If freezing, place cooled meat mixture in freezer bags and freeze, using freezer bag method.

Nutritional Information, option one (per serving): Calories 330.5; Total Fat 26.9g; Cholesterol 85.7mg, Sodium 498.5mg; Total Carbohydrates 4.1g (Dietary Fiber 1.0g); Protein 18.5g

Nutritional Information, option two (per serving): Calories 346.8; Total Fat 26.9g; Cholesterol 85.8mg, Sodium 395.1mg; Total Carbohydrates 8.1g (Dietary Fiber 2.4g); Protein 17.5g

Beef and Cashew Stir-Fry

The hoisin gives this classic dish exceptional taste!

Sauce

½ cup chicken broth

1 T. cornstarch

1 T. soy sauce

1 T. hoisin sauce

1 T. rice wine

1 lb. sirloin or flank steak, thinly sliced across the grain

¼ cup vegetable oil, divided

2 cloves garlic, minced

1 T. ginger, minced

1 cup broccoli crowns

½ cup snow peas

¼ cup water

2 T. scallions, sliced thin

½ cup carrots

¼ t. salt

¼ t. sugar

½ cup cashews

Recipe Yield	**Prep Time**	**Total Time**
6 servings	20 minutes	25 minutes

Directions

If you would like to serve rice with this meal, begin to cook rice on stovetop. Mix together sauce ingredients and place by stove.

Heat 2 T. vegetable oil in skillet on medium-high heat and sauté steak until just done, about 3–5 minutes. Remove meat from pan and set aside; wipe out skillet. Add remaining 2 T. vegetable oil to skillet and let heat, then add garlic, ginger, broccoli, snow peas, ¼ cup of prepared sauce, and ¼ cup of water to skillet. Cook for 3–5 minutes or until vegetables become tender.

Add scallions, carrots, salt, and sugar to skillet and cook for 2 more minutes. Add steak and remaining sauce to skillet and cook for 1–2 more minutes or just until thickened. Sprinkle cashews over stir-fry just prior to serving.

Nutritional Information (per serving): Calories 346.8; Total Fat 21.0g; Cholesterol 67.7mg; Sodium 470.9mg; Total Carbohydrates 13.3g (Dietary Fiber 1.9g); Protein 26.1g

Beef Sauté with Mushroom Wine Sauce

A gourmet dish prepared in minutes.

1 lb. sirloin, cut into ¼-inch strips
½ t. salt, divided
¼ t. pepper
¼ t. garlic salt
2 T. olive oil, divided
1–10 oz. pkg. mushrooms, sliced
1 large shallot, minced
½ cup beef broth
½ cup dry red wine
2 T. chopped fresh parsley

Recipe Yield

4 servings

Prep Time

30 minutes

Total Time

30 minutes

Directions

Sprinkle sliced meat with ¼ t. salt, pepper, and garlic salt. In a large nonstick skillet, heat 1 T. olive oil over medium-high heat. Add half the sirloin and cook until browned on both sides, 5–6 minutes. Do not crowd beef or it will boil instead of fry. Transfer meat to platter and cover loosely with foil. Repeat with remaining beef, adding oil as needed.

In the same skillet, add mushrooms, shallot, and remaining ¼ t. salt. Cook, stirring frequently, until mushroom mixture is browned, about 3–4 minutes. Add broth, wine, and juices from meat platter. Cook another 3–4 minutes until sauce is reduced by half, stirring occasionally. Stir in parsley. Pour sauce over meat. Serve with Oven Roasted Potatoes (see page 80).

Nutritional Information (per serving): Calories 319.0; Total Fat 16.0g; Cholesterol 12.0mg; Sodium 421.0mg; Total Carbohydrates 11.2g (Dietary Fiber 0.4g); Protein 35.7g

Best Grilled Burgers

Keep this recipe on hand for your next burger craving.

1 egg
½ cup water
1 pkg. onion soup mix
¼ cup grated parmesan, Romano, or Asiago cheese
2 T. fresh parsley, chopped, or 1 t. dried
2 T. Worcestershire or steak sauce
1 t. garlic powder
½ t. freshly ground black pepper
¼–½ t. red pepper flakes (optional)
2 lbs. 80 percent lean ground beef*

For Serving

8 hamburger buns or kaiser rolls, split and toasted
cheese slices
lettuce leaves
thin tomato slices
thin red onion slices
dill pickle spears

*Using meat that is too lean will produce dry burgers.

Recipe Yield	**Prep Time**	**Total Time**
8 servings	25 minutes	35–45 minutes

Directions

In a large bowl, thoroughly combine egg, water, and onion soup mix. Stir in cheese, parsley, Worcestershire sauce, garlic powder, and pepper. Add ground beef and, using clean hands, gently combine the egg mixture and ground meat until evenly distributed. Handle meat mixture as little as possible for more tender and moist burgers.

Shape meat mixture into 8 patties approximately 4 inches wide.

Grill burgers on the greased rack of an uncovered grill over medium heat for 14–18 minutes or until meat is done. Internal temperature of burgers should reach 160 degrees. Just before removing burgers from grill, top with slice of cheese if desired.

Nutritional Information (per serving): Calories 329.2; Total Fat 25.0g; Cholesterol 114.1mg; Sodium 268.7mg; Total Carbohydrates 2.2g (Dietary Fiber 0.1g); Protein 22.4g

Tip

For a quick cleanup and no messy hands, wear disposable latex gloves when you mix with your hands.

Chicken and Green Olive Stir-Fry

This unique blend of flavors really works together to create AMAZING!

3 cups wide egg noodles
¼ cup almonds, whole
2 T. oil
1 garlic clove, minced
2 boneless, skinless chicken breasts, sliced
¾ cup chicken broth
1 t. cornstarch
¼ cup cooking sherry
½ cup stuffed green olives

Recipe Yield

6 servings

Prep Time

30 minutes

Total Time

30 minutes

Directions

Cook noodles according to package directions. Toast the almonds by placing on a baking sheet in a 300 degree oven until lightly browned, approximately 15 minutes.

Grind toasted almonds in food processor or blender. Set aside. Heat oil and garlic in wok or nonstick skillet over high heat. Add chicken and stir-fry until opaque. Pour broth in pan. Reduce heat and simmer for 15 minutes.

Mix cornstarch, sherry, and ground almonds together. Add to chicken and stir until sauce begins to thicken. Mix in olives. Serve over noodles.

Nutritional Information (per serving): Calories 390.0; Total Fat 10.4g; Cholesterol 15.9mg; Sodium 415.0mg; Total Carbohydrates 56.5g (Dietary Fiber 1.0g); Protein 16.6g

Chicken Fajitas Garcia

A favorite in Bonnie's house!

	x3
3 boneless, skinless chicken breasts, cut into strips	9
Marinade	
1 clove garlic, minced	3
1½ t. season salt	1T + 1½t
1½ t. cumin	1T + 1½t
½ t. chili powder	1½t
½ t. crushed red pepper	1½t
1 T. olive oil	3T
2 T. lime juice	¼c*
Fajitas	
¼ cup olive oil, divided	
1 onion, sliced	
1 green pepper, sliced	
For Serving	
flour tortillas, warmed	
salsa	
cheese	
tomato	
lettuce	
avocado	

*This measurement has been adjusted to accommodate the intensified flavor of acidic ingredients when recipe is made in quantity.

Recipe Yield	**Prep Time**	**Total Time**
6 servings	10 minutes	2 hours 30 minutes

Directions

Combine all marinade ingredients in medium bowl; add chicken and toss to coat. Marinate chicken in refrigerator for 2–3 hours. In medium skillet, heat

2 T. olive oil and sauté onion and green pepper until lightly browned. Remove from pan. Add remaining 2 T. olive oil and sauté chicken and marinade in same skillet until chicken is browned and cooked through, about 10 minutes. Return vegetables to pan and mix until well combined. Spoon fajita mixture into warm flour tortillas and top with favorite ingredients.

Freezing Instructions

To make this recipe x3 and freeze the extra meals, use the quantity table listed for the appropriate ingredient amounts. Place chicken and marinade in freezer bags. Freeze, using freezer bag method. Prepare onion and green pepper on serving day.

Nutritional Information (per serving): Calories 239.0; Total Fat 11.8g; Cholesterol 65.7mg; Sodium 659.8mg; Total Carbohydrates 5.6g (Dietary Fiber 1.1g); Protein 17.0g

Chicken Piccata

A restaurant-style meal in less than 30 minutes.

6 boneless, skinless chicken breasts, pounded thin (or prepackaged thin-cut breasts)
salt and pepper to taste
¼ cup flour
2 T. olive oil
1 T. chopped onion
2 t. chopped garlic
2 T. fresh lemon juice
¼ cup white wine
2 t. capers, drained
½ cup + 2 T. butter

Recipe Yield	**Prep Time**	**Total Time**
4–6 servings	10–15 minutes	30 minutes

Directions

Sprinkle both sides of chicken breasts with salt and pepper. Place flour in a shallow plate and dredge chicken with flour on both sides. Heat olive oil in large sauté pan on medium-high heat. Add onion, garlic, and chicken. Sauté until chicken is cooked through on both sides, about 1 minute each side. Watch that the garlic does not burn. Remove chicken from pan.

Quickly pour lemon juice and white wine into pan. Add capers and butter, scraping up any browned bits. Cook for 1 minute to reduce sauce. Taste, and season with additional salt and pepper if desired. Return chicken to pan, coating each side with sauce, and place on serving plate. Spoon remaining sauce over chicken.

Nutritional Information (per serving): Calories 432.2; Total Fat 29.5g; Cholesterol 152.3mg; Sodium 295.2mg; Total Carbohydrates 0.9g (Dietary Fiber 0.1g); Protein 36.7g

Crispy Chicken Ranch Cutlets or Sandwiches

Crunchy on the outside—so tender on the inside.

⅓ cup flour
½ t. pepper
1–1 oz. pkg. ranch dressing mix, divided
2 eggs
1 t. canola oil
1¼ cups panko breadcrumbs*
1½ lbs. boneless, skinless chicken breast fillets, thin-sliced**
canola oil for pan frying

*Panko breadcrumbs can be found in the Asian/ethnic aisles of most grocery stores or in larger quantities in Asian markets. Panko crumbs are much lighter than regular breadcrumbs and make a crunchier coating when baked or fried.

**Many grocery stores carry prepackaged thin-sliced breasts, but you can quickly thin-slice regular breasts. Slice them no more than ½-inch thick.

Recipe Yield	**Prep Time**	**Total Time**
4–5 chicken cutlets or sandwiches	20–30 minutes	40–50 minutes

Directions

Use 3 separate shallow dishes or pie plates for breading. Place the flour, pepper, and 1½ T. of the dry ranch mix into the first dish. Mix together. In the second dish beat together the eggs and 1 t. oil with fork. In the third dish gently mix together the panko crumbs and the remainder of dry ranch mix (approx. 3 T.). Place a wire cooling rack on top of a cookie sheet and set aside. Preheat oven to 200 degrees. Place an ovenproof plate or baking sheet in the oven while it is preheating.

Dredge chicken cutlet in flour mixture, gently shaking off excess. Using tongs (or see tip below) dip both sides of floured cutlet into the egg mixture, allowing excess to drip back into dish. Then dip both sides of cutlet into panko crumb mixture. Gently press crumbs with fingers to form an even coating on chicken. Place breaded cutlet on wire rack so the coating has a chance to dry for a few minutes before frying. Repeat with remaining cutlets.

In a large nonstick skillet, heat 3–5 T. oil over medium-high heat just until shimmering (not smoking). If oil smokes, it's too hot and will burn the breading. Lay 2–3 cutlets in skillet (overcrowding inhibits crispy browning). Cook until deep golden brown and crisp, approximately 2–2½ minutes. Flip cutlets and immediately reduce heat to medium. Using spatula, press on cutlets to ensure even browning. Cook for an additional 2–3 minutes, until golden brown and crispy. Take pan off heat, and transfer cutlets to paper towel–lined plate/baking sheet in oven. Wipe out any remaining oil in skillet with paper towels and tongs. Add fresh oil to wiped skillet and repeat process for remaining cutlets.

Nutritional Information (per serving): Calories 255.0; Total Fat 9.3g; Cholesterol 109.6mg; Sodium 689.7mg; Total Carbohydrates 29.3g (Dietary Fiber 1.5g); Protein 12.0g

Tip

For a quick cleanup, no messy hands, and no contamination, use disposable latex gloves to bread the chicken. Gloves can be purchased in larger quantity at warehouse club stores and in larger grocery stores.

Dad's Favorite Pork Chops with Mushroom Gravy

Whip up your favorite box stuffing mix for the perfect comfort meal.

4 thick-cut pork chops (or 6 thinner cut)
1 t. salt
½ t. pepper
1–2 T. olive oil
8 oz. fresh mushrooms, sliced thin (or more)
2 T. unsalted butter
2 T. flour
2 cups heavy cream (can substitute table cream)
1 T. flat-leaf Italian parsley, minced (or ½ t. dried)
salt and pepper, to taste

For Serving

1 box of stovetop-type stuffing (pork flavored or your choice)

Recipe Yield	Prep Time	Total Time
4 servings	25–30 minutes	40 minutes

Directions

Sprinkle trimmed pork chops with salt and pepper. Heat olive oil in a heavy skillet over medium heat. Sear pork chops on each side until nicely browned and then cook through, about 6–10 minutes total for thicker chops, less for thinner cuts. While pork chops are cooking, prepare stuffing mix according to package directions.

Take pork chops out of skillet. Place on a plate and cover with foil, allowing them to rest. Preserve any juices that accumulate.

Place mushrooms in same skillet and cook until just golden. Reduce heat; add butter and flour. Cook for 1 minute, then add cream and juices from the cooked pork all at once. Stir constantly until sauce thickens. Remove from heat and sprinkle with parsley. Season with salt and pepper to taste. Serve with pork chops and stuffing.

Nutritional Information (per serving): Calories 533.6; Total Fat 43.3g; Cholesterol 152.7mg; Sodium 515.0mg; Total Carbohydrates 11.5g (Dietary Fiber 0.7g); Protein 26.1g

Fiery Orange Chicken

The red pepper flakes make this Asian dish a winner!

Sauce

2 T. cornstarch
¼ cup cooking sherry
1 cup chicken broth
¼ cup soy sauce
⅓ cup orange marmalade
½ t. crushed red pepper flakes

3 T. canola oil
1 lb. boneless, skinless chicken breasts, sliced thin*
¼ cup grated orange peel
1 clove garlic, minced
½ t. ginger

roasted salted peanuts, for garnish (optional)

*Many grocery stores carry prepackaged thin-sliced breasts, but you can quickly thin-slice regular breasts. Slice them no more than ½-inch thick.

Recipe Yield

4 servings

Prep Time

40 minutes

Total Time

40 minutes

Directions

Mix together sauce ingredients, stirring until smooth, and place by stove. In a large skillet or wok, heat canola oil over medium-high heat. Add chicken strips in 2–3 batches, adding more oil between batches as needed. Cook each batch for 3–4 minutes until chicken is brown and no longer pink, then move to platter. Return all of chicken to skillet. Add orange peel, garlic, and ginger. Continue to stir-fry for an additional minute. Add sauce to chicken mixture. Bring to boil, and continue boiling for 3–4 minutes, stirring, until sauce is thickened.

Serve with rice and top with peanuts if desired.

Nutritional Information (per serving): Calories 285.0; Total Fat 7.7g; Cholesterol 56.2mg; Sodium 1385.6mg; Total Carbohydrates 26.5g (Dietary Fiber 1.2g); Protein 24.6g

Mexican Carne Asada Stir-Fry

A Mexican tradition in a skillet.

| 1–1½ lbs. skirt steak or sirloin steak |
| 1 large onion, diced |
| 1–4 oz. can green chiles, chopped (or ½ cup freshly roasted green chiles, chopped) |
| 2 T. canola oil |

Marinade

| 3 T. canola or olive oil |
| 2 T. water |
| 1 T. chili powder |
| 1 T. ground cumin |
| 1 t. brown sugar |
| ¼ t. red chili flakes |
| 1½ t. pepper |
| ½ t. garlic salt |
| ½ t. salt |
| 1 t. dried oregano |

Toppings

| 8–12 corn or flour tortillas, fajita size |
| lettuce or cabbage, finely shredded |
| tomatoes, chopped |
| avocado slices |
| cheese, shredded (cheddar or Mexican blend) |
| lime wedges |
| sour cream |
| salsa |

Recipe Yield

4–6 servings

Prep Time

20 minutes

Total Time

40–50 minutes

Directions

Cut steak into fairly small pieces. Place meat and diced onion into freezer bag or baking dish.

Mix all marinade ingredients together in a small bowl, adding 1–2 T. of water to thin marinade if needed. Pour over meat and onions and mix well. (If using freezer bag, you can simply seal the bag and knead to distribute marinade throughout the meat.) Allow meat to marinate for at least 15–20 minutes. While meat is marinating, prepare the toppings. Tortillas can be heated in oven and wrapped in foil to keep warm.

Heat a heavy skillet over medium to medium-high heat. Add 1–2 T. oil to coat bottom and sides of pan. Working in 2 batches, place meat mixture and green chiles in hot skillet, stir-frying quickly to make sure meat is evenly cooked, about 3–5 minutes. Do not crowd the meat, or it will boil instead of fry. Add more oil between batches if needed. Serve immediately on warm corn or flour tortillas with a squeeze of lime and your choice of toppings.

Nutritional Information (per serving): Calories 365.0; Total Fat 22.8g; Cholesterol 0.0mg; Sodium 35.8mg; Total Carbohydrates 2.2g (Dietary Fiber .5g); Protein 35.0g

Pecan Crusted Fish

A succulent fish with a crunchy crust.

4–6 oz. fish fillets such as tilapia, snapper, cod, or halibut

Crust

1 cup breadcrumbs or panko breadcrumbs*

¼ cup pecans, finely chopped (or pistachios)

½ t. garlic powder

¼ t. cayenne pepper

1 t. salt

½ t. pepper

½ cup low-fat buttermilk

1 t. hot sauce

3–4 T. flour

¼ cup vegetable or olive oil

4 lemon/lime wedges for serving

*Panko breadcrumbs can be found in the Asian/ethnic aisles of most grocery stores or in larger quantities in Asian markets. Panko crumbs are much lighter than regular breadcrumbs and make a crunchier coating when baked or fried.

Recipe Yield	**Prep Time**	**Total Time**
4–6 servings	30 minutes	30 minutes

Directions

Blot fish fillets with paper towel. Combine crust ingredients in a shallow baking dish or pie plate. Combine buttermilk and hot sauce in bowl. Place flour in a separate shallow dish or pie plate (see tip on next page). Dredge fillet in flour, then dip into buttermilk mixture, and finally dip into crust mixture. Repeat with remaining fillets.

In a large nonstick skillet, heat 1 T. oil over medium heat. Add fillets, working in 2 batches if necessary—don't crowd fish. Cook 3 minutes on each side or just until fish easily flakes with fork. Repeat with remaining fillets, adding more oil as needed. Serve with a squeeze of fresh lemon or lime.

Nutritional Information (per serving): Calories 130.8; Total Fat 4.7g; Cholesterol 0.2mg; Sodium 739.6mg; Total Carbohydrates 18.6g (Dietary Fiber 1.6g); Protein 3.9g

Tip

For a quick cleanup and no messy hands, use disposable latex gloves to bread the fish. They can be purchased in larger quantity at warehouse club stores and in larger grocery stores.

Pineapple Sun Pork Stir-Fry

A hot Hawaiian dish!

1–20 oz. can pineapple chunks in juice
½ cup water
3 T. soy sauce
1 T. cornstarch
1 t. white vinegar
¼ t. hot pepper flakes
2 T. oil
1 lb. boneless pork
2 large cloves garlic
2 T. minced ginger root or 1 t. ground ginger
2 medium carrots, sliced thin
1 onion, cut into wedges
1 green or red pepper, cut in bite-sized pieces
2 cups snow peas

Recipe Yield

8 servings

Prep Time

25 minutes

Total Time

35 minutes

Directions

Drain pineapple, reserving 3 T. juice. Mix reserved juice with ½ cup water, soy sauce, cornstarch, vinegar, and pepper flakes; set aside. Heat oil in wok or nonstick skillet. Cut pork into thin strips and brown in hot oil. Add garlic and ginger and cook 1 minute. Add carrots and onion; cook 1 minute. Stir sauce until smooth and then add to skillet with pineapple, peppers, and snow peas. Cook until sauce thickens and vegetables are crisp-tender. Serve with rice.

Nutritional Information (per serving): Calories 168.0; Total Fat 8.4g; Cholesterol 44.8mg; Sodium 376.3mg; Total Carbohydrates 5.9g (Dietary Fiber 0.3g); Protein 16.2g

Saucy Skillet Sirloin

Wonderful served with Oven Roasted Potatoes!

	x3
1½ lbs. sirloin steak, cut into thin strips	4½ lbs
¼ cup flour	¾c
¾ t. salt	2¼t
¼ t. pepper	¾t
½ medium onion, sliced	1½
2 T. olive oil	¼c + 2T
1 T. molasses	3T
3 T. soy sauce	½c +1T
1 cup beef broth	3c
1–14.5 oz. can diced tomatoes, undrained	3

Recipe Yield

4 servings

Prep Time

25 minutes

Total Time

1 hour 10 minutes

Directions

In a shallow bowl, mix together flour, salt, and pepper. Toss steak strips in flour mixture. Heat olive oil in a large skillet over medium-high heat, then add steak and onion. Brown steak in oil for 3–5 minutes. Add remaining ingredients to skillet. Bring to a boil, then reduce heat, cover, and continue to simmer for 45–50 minutes or until sauce is thickened and steak is tender. Wonderful served with roasted potatoes, rice, or noodles!

Freezing Instructions

To make this recipe x3 and freeze the extra meals, use the quantity table listed for the appropriate ingredient amounts. Prepare the meal as directed above. Cool completely. Place in freezer bags in serving-size portions. Freeze, using freezer bag method. On serving day, thaw and reheat on stovetop.

Nutritional Information (per serving): Calories 179.0; Total Fat 8.2g; Cholesterol 0.0mg; Sodium 1580.2mg; Total Carbohydrates 17.4g (Dietary Fiber 1.6g); Protein 9.6g

Spicy Shrimp and Asparagus Stir-Fry

A great quick dish for shrimp lovers!

Stir-Fry Ingredients

1 cup asparagus, cut into 1-inch pieces
2 T. peanut or vegetable oil, divided
2 cloves garlic, minced
1 t. fresh ginger, minced or grated
2 T. scallions, minced
pinch salt
¾ cup mushrooms, sliced or quartered
1 lb. medium or large shrimp, peeled and deveined

Spicy Sauce

¾ cup chicken broth
1 T. cornstarch
2 T. soy sauce
2 T. rice vinegar or dry sherry
½ t. sesame oil
1 T. sugar
2 t. chili sauce (Asian if available)

Recipe Yield	**Prep Time**	**Total Time**
6 servings	20 minutes	20 minutes

Directions

Steam asparagus on stove or cook for 1–2 minutes on high in the microwave. Prepare all stir-fry ingredients and place by stove. Mix together ingredients for spicy sauce and set aside.

Heat 2 T. oil in wok or nonstick skillet. Add asparagus, garlic, ginger, scallions, salt, and mushrooms and stir-fry for 1–2 minutes.

Add shrimp and cook 1 minute longer. Add spicy sauce and cook, stirring, until sauce is thickened and all ingredients are cooked through, about 3 minutes. Serve with rice.

Nutritional Information (per serving): Calories 140.0; Total Fat 6.2g; Cholesterol 148.0mg; Sodium 590.0mg; Total Carbohydrates 3.8g (Dietary Fiber 0.7g); Protein 17.0g

Sweet and Sour Pork Stir-Fry

Yes, you can make sweet and sour dishes at home!

Stir-Fry Ingredients

5 T. peanut or vegetable oil, divided

1 lb. pork tenderloin, thinly sliced

2 cloves garlic, minced

1 t. fresh ginger, minced

2 scallions, minced

pinch salt

½ cup carrots, sliced

½ cup green pepper, cut into bite-sized pieces

¼ cup pineapple tidbits or chunks

¼ cup water chestnuts, sliced

Sweet and Sour Sauce

¾ cup chicken broth

2 t. cornstarch

¼ cup ketchup

2 t. soy sauce

3 T. rice vinegar

¼ cup sugar

½ t. salt

1 t. sesame oil

Recipe Yield	**Prep Time**	**Total Time**
6 servings	25 minutes	30 minutes

Directions

Prepare all stir-fry ingredients and place by stove. Combine ingredients for sweet and sour sauce and set aside. Heat 3 T. oil in wok or nonstick skillet.

Add pork and cook until just opaque, 3–4 minutes. Transfer to a plate and set aside. Discard oil in pan and wipe pan with a paper towel.

Heat pan on high for 1–2 minutes and add 2 T. fresh oil to pan. Add garlic, ginger, scallions, and salt and stir-fry 30 seconds. Add carrots and green pepper; stir-fry 30 more seconds. Add pineapple and water chestnuts; stir-fry until all ingredients are crisp-tender, about 3–5 minutes.

Add the cooked pork and sweet and sour sauce to pan, and cook, stirring, until sauce is thickened and all ingredients are cooked through, about 3 minutes. Serve with rice.

Nutritional Information (per serving): Calories 281.0; Total Fat 15.0g; Cholesterol 51.7mg; Sodium 310.0mg; Total Carbohydrates 15.4g (Dietary Fiber 2.3g); Protein 19.7g

Thai Beef with Rice Noodles

For when you're craving Thai . . .

¾ lb. sirloin
8 oz. dried rice noodles
1 t. vegetable oil

Sauce

¼ cup soy sauce
2 T. fish sauce*
2 T. brown sugar
¼ t. black pepper

5 T. vegetable oil, divided
1 T. garlic, minced
1 lb. greens, such as baby spinach or bok choy cut into ½-inch strips
2 eggs, beaten
¼ t. crushed dried red pepper flakes

For Serving

rice vinegar to taste (optional)
fresh basil or mint leaves, for garnish

*Fish sauce maybe found in the Asian section of the grocery store.

Recipe Yield	**Prep Time**	**Total Time**
4 servings	20–25 minutes	40–45 minutes

Directions

Slice sirloin into 2-inch long, ¼-inch wide strips. Set aside. Place noodles in medium bowl and add 1 t. oil. Add warm water to cover; let sit 5 minutes, then drain. In a small bowl combine the sauce ingredients; set aside.

Heat a wok or heavy skillet over medium-high heat. Add 2 T. vegetable oil. When oil is hot but not smoking, add the garlic and cook, stirring constantly, for 5 seconds. Add the greens and stir-fry approximately 2 minutes. Remove greens and garlic from skillet and set aside.

Make sure the skillet is still hot and add 1–2 T. more oil. Add sirloin and stir-fry until meat is browned on all sides, about 2 minutes. Remove from skillet and set aside.

Heat a little more oil in skillet and add noodles. Toss until warmed through, approximately 2 minutes; set aside.

Heat the remaining oil in skillet. Quickly add the eggs and cook, without stirring, until they are set, about 30 seconds. Break up eggs slightly and stir back in noodles, beef, greens, and red pepper flakes. Stir in the sauce, tossing to coat, and heat through. Serve immediately; sprinkle with rice vinegar and chopped basil or mint leaves to taste.

Nutritional Information (per serving): Calories 391.4; Total Fat 21.1g; Cholesterol 161.7mg; Sodium 1555.5mg; Total Carbohydrates 22.6g (Dietary Fiber 2.1g); Protein 29.4g

Desserts Divine

Bittersweet Chocolate Glazed Tart
Brown Sugar Shortbread
Butter Walnut Blondies
Chocolate Buttercream Frosting
Chocolate Chip Cookies in a Jar
Chocolate Cream Pie
Crazy Good Chocolate Cake
Dipped Gingersnaps
Fruit Pizza
Homemade Caramel Toppings
Homemade Trail Mix
Marvelous Lemon Bars
Mexican Chocolate Mousse
Pecan Tart with Oatmeal Crust
Quick Apple Pie Wedges
Ruth's Hot Fudge Sauce
Sour Cream Cookies
Tiramisu
White Chocolate Pudding with
  Strawberries

Bittersweet Chocolate Glazed Tart

The best chocolate dessert you will ever taste . . . very easy to make. Declared a pain reliever by Susie's friend Laurel!

Crust*

1 cup chocolate graham crackers, finely ground

5 T. unsalted butter, melted

¼ cup sugar

Filling

1¼ cups heavy cream

9 oz. bittersweet chocolate (not more than 65% cacao), chopped

2 large eggs

1 t. pure vanilla

¼ t. salt

Glaze

2 T. heavy cream

1¾ oz. bittersweet chocolate, finely chopped

1 t. light corn syrup

1 T. warm water

*You can substitute a store-bought chocolate graham pie shell, if desired.

Recipe Yield	**Prep Time**	**Total Time**
10–12 servings	30 minutes	2¼ hours (includes cooling)

Directions

Preheat oven to 350 degrees, with rack in the middle.

For crust: stir together all crust ingredients and press onto bottom and up the sides of a 9-inch tart pan. Bake until firm, about 10 minutes; allow to cool on a rack. If using purchased crust, bake for only 5 minutes.

For filling: bring cream to a boil in a medium saucepan and immediately remove from stove. Place chocolate in a medium bowl and pour hot cream over chocolate; let stand 5 minutes. Gently stir until smooth. In another bowl whisk together eggs, vanilla, and salt, then stir into melted chocolate. Pour filling into cooled crust. Bake at 350 degrees until filling is set about 3 inches from edge but very center of tart is still wobbly, 20–25 minutes. (Center will continue to set as tart cools.) Cool completely in pan on rack, about 40 minutes.

For glaze: bring cream to a boil in a small saucepan. Remove from heat. Stir in chocolate until smooth. Stir in corn syrup, then warm water. Pour glaze onto tart, then carefully tilt and rotate tart so glaze coats top evenly. Let stand until glaze is set.

Nutritional Information (per serving): Calories 327.9; Total Fat 21.6g; Cholesterol 82.0mg; Sodium 96.5mg; Total Carbohydrates 36.9g (Dietary Fiber 2.5g); Protein 4.6g

Brown Sugar Shortbread

*An elegant but easy shortbread cookie
using only four ingredients!*

Contributed by AnnMarie Moseley—Highlands Ranch, Colorado

	x3
1 cup butter, softened	3c
½ cup brown sugar	1½c
2¼ cups flour	6¾c
granulated sugar for sprinkling	

Recipe Yield	Prep Time	Total Time
24 cookies	30 minutes	1 hour

Directions

Preheat oven to 300 degrees. Mix butter and sugar together with an electric mixer until well blended. Add flour a little at a time. Mixture will be a coarse crumb consistency. Knead dough onto a lightly floured surface until smooth. Roll out dough fairly thick (about ¼ inch). Cut into small shapes with cookie cutters. (These cookies are rich, so small shapes are better!) Place cookies on ungreased cookie sheets and bake for 25–30 minutes. Do not let cookies turn brown. Immediately sprinkle cookies with granulated sugar on both sides when removed from oven. Cool on rack.

> **Hint**
>
> These are great cookies for sharing! The ingredients are ones you usually have on hand, the cookies store beautifully, and people will really think you have fussed to make them. Wonderful for any holiday or season!

Freezing Instructions

To make this recipe x3 and freeze the extra dough, use the quantity table listed for the appropriate ingredient amounts. Form cookie dough into logs, wrap in plastic wrap, and place logs in freezer bag. Freeze, using freezer bag method. On baking day, thaw dough and continue as directed.

Nutritional Information (per cookie): Calories 135.8; Total Fat 7.8g; Cholesterol 20.3mg; Sodium 56.5mg; Total Carbohydrates 17.1g (Dietary Fiber 0.3g); Protein 1.3g

Butter Walnut Blondies

You will not be able to stop eating these! Serve alone or get fancy with ice cream and caramel topping.

1 cup walnut pieces, divided
2 cups flour
1 t. baking powder
½ t. baking soda
1 t. salt
½ cup + 2 T. unsalted butter, softened
1½ cups packed light brown sugar
3 large eggs
2 T. vanilla extract
6 oz. white chocolate, cut into chunks

Recipe Yield

12 servings

Prep Time

20 minutes

Total Time

50 minutes

Directions

Preheat oven to 350 degrees. Line a 9 x 13 pan with parchment paper. Pulse ½ cup walnuts in a food processor or blender until almost fine (do not over-process). Whisk ground walnuts, flour, baking powder, baking soda, and salt together in a medium bowl.

With a mixer, beat butter and brown sugar in a medium bowl until fluffy, about 2 minutes. Beat in eggs one at a time, scraping the bowl after each egg is incorporated. Beat in vanilla. Gradually mix in dry ingredients just until combined (do not overbeat). Fold in white chocolate chunks and remaining ½ cup walnuts.

Spread batter in prepared pan and bake until blondies are light brown around the edges and spring back when pressed with finger, about 30 minutes. Cool on rack. Cut into 3 x 3 inch bars.

Serve with ice cream and Maple Caramel Topping found on page 230.

Freezing Instructions

To freeze blondies, individually wrap squares and place in freezer bags. Freeze, using freezer bag method, for up to 3 months.

Nutritional Information (per serving): Calories 464.0; Total Fat 25.7; Cholesterol 285.3mg; Sodium 383.0mg; Total Carbohydrates 55.7g (Dietary Fiber 1.5g); Protein 12.0g

Chocolate Buttercream Frosting

A scrumptious frosting, great on your favorite cake!

6 T. butter, softened
¾ cup cocoa
2⅔ cups powdered sugar
⅓ cup milk
1 t. vanilla

Recipe Yield	**Prep Time**	**Total Time**
Frosting for a 2-layer round cake or 9 x 13 sheet cake	10 minutes	15 minutes

Directions

Cream butter in medium bowl with an electric mixer. Add cocoa and continue mixing until well blended. Alternately add powdered sugar and milk to butter mixture, blending well after each addition. Beat until frosting is a smooth spreading consistency. Blend in vanilla. Frost cake and enjoy!

Nutritional Information (per ¼ cup serving): Calories 123.0; Total Fat 4.4g; Cholesterol 10.2mg; Sodium 30.7mg; Total Carbohydrates 22.3g (Dietary Fiber 1.3g); Protein 1.0g

Chocolate Chip Cookies in a Jar

This recipe involves making a dry cookie mix,
then assembling the mix and chocolate chip cookie
ingredients in decorative canning jars.
Makes a wonderful housewarming or holiday gift!

Basic Cookie Mix

8 cups flour
2½ cups sugar
2 cups brown sugar, firmly packed
4 t. salt
1½ t. baking soda
3 cups shortening

Yield

5 quart jars of Chocolate Chip Cookie Mix

Directions for Cookie Mix

In a large bowl, combine flour, sugar, brown sugar, salt, and soda until well blended. With a pastry blender, cut in shortening until evenly distributed. Place in a large, airtight container. Store in a cool, dry place and use within 10–12 weeks. Makes about 15 cups of Basic Cookie Mix.

Directions for Assembling Chocolate Chip Cookie Jars

In a 1 quart canning jar, layer as follows: 1 cup Basic Cookie Mix, 1 cup chocolate chips, 1 cup cookie mix, ½ cup chopped nuts, and 1 cup cookie mix. Cover with canning lid and/or decorative cover. Attach baking instructions (see below) and give to a friend!

Directions for Baking Chocolate Chip Cookie Mix

Preheat oven to 375 degrees. Pour all dry ingredients from canning jar into a large bowl. Add 3 T. milk, 1 t. vanilla, and 1 egg. Stir until mixed. Drop by teaspoonfuls onto a greased baking sheet. Bake for 10–15 minutes, until golden brown. Enjoy!

Recipe Yield	Prep Time	Total Time
24 cookies	10 minutes	25 minutes

Nutritional Information (per cookie): Calories 145.0; Total Fat 8.2g; Cholesterol 12.9mg; Sodium 93.8mg; Total Carbohydrates 18.0g (Dietary Fiber 0.7g); Protein 1.9g

Chocolate Cream Pie

A chocolate pudding pie . . . thick, rich, and full of flavor!

Crust

1 graham cracker piecrust

Filling

2 large egg yolks

½ cup sugar

3 T. cornstarch

3 cups whole milk

5 oz. bittersweet or semisweet chocolate, chopped

pinch salt

1 T. vanilla extract

Cinnamon Cream

1 cup heavy cream

1 T. sugar

¼ t. ground cinnamon

Recipe Yield	**Prep Time**	**Total Time**
6–8 servings	30 minutes	2 hours 30 minutes

Directions

To make filling: whisk egg yolks, sugar, and cornstarch in a large bowl. Combine milk, chocolate, and salt in a saucepan over medium heat and stir until the chocolate melts. Cool slightly (1 minute). Gradually pour the chocolate mixture into the egg mixture, whisking constantly. Pour filling back into saucepan and cook on low heat until thick, about 12–15 minutes. Remove from heat and stir in vanilla. Cool filling for 5 minutes, then stir and pour into piecrust. Cover with plastic wrap and refrigerate for 2 hours.

For cinnamon cream: whip cream and sugar in a mixing bowl until it just holds soft peaks; fold in the cinnamon. Serve pie with a dollop of cinnamon cream on each piece.

Nutritional Information (per serving): Calories 284.2; Total Fat 17.9g; Cholesterol 84.4mg; Sodium 90.6mg; Total Carbohydrates 27.6g (Dietary Fiber 0.3g); Protein 4.7g

Crazy Good Chocolate Cake

Can you say RICH DARK CHOCOLATE? No frosting on this one—a dusting of powdered sugar is all you need!

1½ cups flour
1 cup sugar
⅓ cup unsweetened cocoa powder
1 t. baking soda
½ t. salt
1 cup cold water
⅓ cup vegetable oil
1 T. distilled white vinegar
1 t. vanilla

Recipe Yield   **Prep Time**   **Total Time**

8 servings   15 minutes   45 minutes

Directions

Preheat oven to 350 degrees. Place first five ingredients in an 8 x 8 x 2 nonstick metal pan. Using handle of a wooden spoon, poke 3 holes in dry ingredients. Combine cold water, oil, vinegar, and vanilla in a large glass measuring cup. Pour liquid ingredients into three holes in dry ingredients (there will be some overflow). Using a fork, stir gently until batter is smooth. Bake until toothpick inserted in center comes out clean, about 30 minutes. Cool completely in pan on rack.

Dust with powdered sugar and serve . . . no frosting needed on this delicious snack!

Nutritional Information (per serving): Calories: 271.8; Total Fat 9.7g; Cholesterol 0mg; Sodium 304.5mg; Total Carbohydrates 44.9g (Dietary Fiber 1.8g); Protein 3.1g

Dipped Gingersnaps

When the air is crisp outside,
these will warm you up inside!

2 cups sugar
1½ cups vegetable oil
2 eggs
1 t. vanilla
½ cup molasses (light)
4 cups flour
1 T. baking soda
1 T. ground ginger
2 t. ground cinnamon
¼ t. cloves
1 t. salt

½ cup sugar (for rolling cookie dough balls)
2–12 oz. pkgs. vanilla baking chips
¼ cup shortening

Recipe Yield

6 dozen cookies

Prep Time

15–20 minutes

Total Time

60 minutes

Directions

Preheat oven to 350 degrees. Combine sugar and oil in a large mixing bowl and mix well. Add eggs one at a time, beating well after each addition. Stir in vanilla and molasses. In medium mixing bowl, combine remaining dry ingredients and gradually add to sugar mixture; mix well. Shape into ¾-inch balls and roll in sugar. Place 2 inches apart on ungreased baking sheets. Bake for 10–12 minutes or until cookies spring back when touched lightly. Move to wire racks to cool.

For dipping: melt vanilla chips with shortening in small saucepan over low heat, stirring constantly. Dip each cookie halfway; gently shake off excess. Place cookies on waxed paper–lined baking sheets until dip hardens. Store in airtight container between layers of waxed paper.

Nutritional Information (per 3 cookies): Calories 440.7; Total Fat 54.6g; Cholesterol 17.7mg; Sodium 265.8mg; Total Carbohydrates 55.8g (Dietary Fiber 82.0g); Protein 3.9g

Fruit Pizza

Two variations satisfy the cravings of chocolate
and sugar cookie lovers alike!

Sugar Cookie Crust

½ cup butter, softened
½ cup sugar
1 egg
½ t. vanilla
1½ cups flour
1 t. cream of tartar
½ t. baking powder

Filling

2–8 oz. pkgs. cream cheese, softened
⅔ cup sugar

Topping

1–8 oz. can crushed pineapple, drained
2 bananas, sliced
2 cups strawberries, sliced

Recipe Yield	**Prep Time**	**Total Time**
12 servings	30 minutes	40 minutes

Directions

To make crust: in mixing bowl, beat together butter and sugar until well blended. Add egg and beat until light yellow. Add vanilla. In a separate bowl, mix together flour, cream of tartar, and baking powder. Gradually add dry ingredients to butter mixture. Mix on low speed until blended. Pat dough into greased 14-inch pizza pan and bake at 400 degrees for 8 minutes. Cool completely.

To *make filling*: beat cream cheese on medium speed until smooth. Add sugar and blend. Spread onto cooled cookie crust. Top with pineapple, bananas, and strawberries. Slice into wedges and serve immediately.

Nutritional Information (per serving): Calories 342; Total Fat 14.5g; Cholesterol 60mg; Sodium 257.3mg; Total Carbohydrates 42.4g (Dietary Fiber 1.7g); Protein 11.8g

Hint

For a chocolate lover's variation, substitute the sugar cookie crust with a brownie crust. Purchase a 21 oz. brownie mix and mix according to package directions. Pour batter into greased 14-inch pizza pan and bake at 350 degrees for 15–20 minutes until set. Cool completely. Complete pizza with filling and topping as directed.

Homemade Caramel Toppings

*Great for ice cream, blondies, and dipping apples
or any other favorite fruit!*

Maple Syrup Caramel

⅓ cup maple syrup
6 T. unsalted butter
¼ cup heavy cream

Recipe Yield	Prep Time	Total Time
1 ¼ cups	12 minutes	12 minutes

Directions

Place the maple syrup and butter in a small saucepan over medium heat and cook, swirling the pan, until the mixture bubbles and thickens, about 6 minutes. Add cream and continue to cook until topping reaches desired consistency. Serve warm or at room temperature.

Traditional Caramel Syrup

1½ cups sugar
½ cup water
3 T. unsalted butter
1 cup heavy cream

Recipe Yield	Prep Time	Total Time
3 cups	15 minutes	15 minutes

Directions

Stir sugar and water in large, heavy saucepan over medium-low heat until sugar dissolves. Increase heat to medium; boil without stirring until syrup turns deep amber, occasionally swirling pan and brushing down sides of pan with pastry brush dipped in water, about 12 minutes. Remove from heat. Whisk in butter. Gradually add cream (mixture will bubble vigorously). Return to low heat; cook and stir until smooth.

Nutritional Information (per ¼ cup Maple Caramel): Calories 220.0; Total Fat 18.8g; Cholesterol 33.0mg; Sodium 6.6mg; Total Carbohydrates 13.3g (Dietary Fiber 0.7g); Protein 1.7g

Nutritional Information (per ¼ cup Traditional Caramel): Calories 190.0; Total Fat 10.2g; Cholesterol 34.0mg; Sodium 7.2mg; Total Carbohydrates 25.6g (Dietary Fiber 0.0g); Protein 4.0g

Homemade Trail Mix

For a healthy anytime snack—great for on the go!

⅓ cup raw pumpkin seeds (without shell)
¼ cup raw sunflower seeds (without shell)
½ cup raw almonds or pecans
½ cup flake coconut
⅓ cup maple syrup
⅔ cup packed brown sugar
1 T. honey
3 T. vegetable oil
1½ t. ground cinnamon (optional)
2 cups rolled oats
¼ t. salt, or more to taste
1 cup dried cranberries or dried cherries (or other dried fruit of your choice)
1 cup semisweet or white chocolate chips

Recipe Yield

6–8 servings

Prep Time

20 minutes

Total Time

45–50 minutes

Directions

Preheat oven to 350 degrees. Spread pumpkin seeds, sunflower seeds, almonds, and coconut flakes on a baking sheet. Bake for 8–10 minutes until lightly toasted. Set aside to cool.

Reduce oven temperature to 325 degrees. Spray a baking sheet with nonstick cooking spray or line with foil. Set aside.

In a small saucepan, combine maple syrup, brown sugar, honey, oil, and cinnamon over medium heat. Cook, stirring constantly, until sugar has dissolved.

In a large bowl, mix together rolled oats, nut mixture, and salt. Pour maple mixture over oat mixture and stir until combined. Spread onto prepared baking sheet. Bake for 20 minutes. Stir and bake for another 20 minutes, or until brown and crunchy. Remove mix from baking sheet and stir in dried fruit. Cool completely. Once mixture is cool, add chocolate chips. Store in airtight container.

Nutritional Information (per ½ cup serving): Calories 275.3; Total Fat 14.6g; Cholesterol 0.0mg; Sodium 50.0mg; Total Carbohydrates 39.6g (Dietary Fiber 3.2g); Protein 3.2g

Marvelous Lemon Bars

A favorite in the Martinez home that sometimes wins over chocolate—unbelievable!

Crust

¾ cup (1½ sticks) cold, unsalted butter, diced

2 cups flour

¼ cup packed brown sugar

¼ cup powdered sugar

¼ t. salt

Filling

4 large eggs

2 egg yolks

2 cups sugar

⅓ cup flour

½ t. grated lemon zest

¼ t. lemon oil (optional)

1 cup fresh lemon juice (about 8 lemons) or purchased lemon juice

powdered sugar for dusting

Recipe Yield	**Prep Time**	**Total Time**
24 servings	30 minutes	1 hour 15 minutes

Directions

For crust: preheat oven to 350 degrees with rack in the middle position. Grease 9 x 13 pan with vegetable oil and line with parchment paper. Pulse butter, flour, both sugars, and salt in food processor or mixer until dough comes together, about 1 minute. Press dough into pan about ½ inch up the sides. Bake until crust is golden, about 25 minutes. Remove crust from oven and reduce oven temperature to 300 degrees.

For filling: whisk whole eggs, egg yolks, sugar, and flour in bowl until smooth. Whisk in lemon zest, oil, and juice. Pour filling over warm crust and return to oven. Bake until filling is just set, 30–35 minutes.

Let bars cool in pan on rack then refrigerate until firm, approximately 2 hours. Lift out of pan and slice. Dust with powdered sugar before serving.

Nutritional Information (per bar): Calories 238.0; Total Fat 10.3g; Cholesterol 207.0mg; Sodium 77.0mg; Total Carbohydrates 31.1g (Dietary Fiber 0.5g); Protein 6.6g

Mexican Chocolate Mousse

A whole new mousse experience! You will taste the chocolate first, then a kick of cinnamon follows . . . yum!

18.6 oz. (1 box) Mexican chocolate, chopped
½ cup whole milk
¾ t. salt
4 cups chilled heavy whipping cream, divided

Recipe Yield

12 servings

Prep Time

20 minutes

Total Time

40 minutes

Directions

Combine chocolate, milk, and salt in heavy, medium saucepan over medium heat, stirring constantly, until chocolate is dissolved and no longer grainy, about 10 minutes. Transfer chocolate to large bowl. Cool to room temperature.

Using a mixer, beat 3 cups cream in large bowl until soft peaks form. Working in two batches, fold whipped cream into chocolate mixture. Divide chocolate mousse among 12 stemmed glasses or 12 small dessert dishes (about ¾ cup each). Beat remaining cup of cream until soft peaks form. Place a dollop of whipped cream atop each dish of mousse. Chill until ready to serve.

Nutritional Information (per serving): Calories 160.8; Total Fat 15.4g; Cholesterol 58.1mg; Sodium 177.0mg; Total Carbohydrates 3.5g (Dietary Fiber 0.1g); Protein 1.6g

Pecan Tart with Oatmeal Crust

This is similar to a pecan pie—only better!

Crust

½ cup butter, softened

¼ cup sugar

1 cup flour

¾ cup rolled oats

Filling

2 eggs

½ cup light corn syrup

⅔ cup brown sugar

¼ cup butter, melted

1 t. vanilla

1 cup coarsely chopped pecans

⅔ cup rolled oats

8 pecan halves

Recipe Yield

10 servings

Prep Time

20 minutes

Total Time

1 hours 30 minutes

Directions

Heat oven to 350 degrees.

For crust: beat butter and sugar together until fluffy. Combine flour and ¾ cup oats; stir into butter mixture to form crust. Press crust onto bottom and sides of a 9-inch tart pan or pie plate. Bake 20–25 minutes or until golden brown. Cool completely.

For filling: beat eggs, corn syrup, brown sugar, melted butter, and vanilla until blended. Stir in chopped pecans and remaining ⅔ cup oats. Pour into crust. Decorate top with pecan halves. Bake an additional 25–30 minutes or until filling is set.

Nutritional Information (per serving): Calories 369.0; Total Fat 20.4g; Cholesterol 92.9mg; Sodium 161.0mg; Total Carbohydrates 44.5g (Dietary Fiber 2.5g); Protein 8.1g

Quick Apple Pie Wedges

Impressive—so easy and so good!

1–9 inch refrigerated piecrust (such as Pillsbury)
2 medium Granny Smith apples, peeled and cored
¼ cup sugar
1 T. ground cinnamon, plus extra for dusting
pinch nutmeg
whipped cream topping

Recipe Yield

4 servings

Prep Time

25–30 minutes

Total Time

1 hour 10 minutes

Directions

Preheat oven to 400 degrees and place rack in center of oven. Line a baking sheet with parchment paper and spray with vegetable cooking spray. (If you don't have parchment paper, just spray baking sheet with cooking spray.)

On a flat surface, unroll the piecrust. Cut dough into quarters, and then cut quarters in half again so you have 8 wedges. Arrange wedges on prepared baking sheet. Using a fork, prick the pastries all over. Bake until golden brown and crispy, 8–10 minutes. Carefully remove to a wire rack and cool completely, about 10 minutes.

Slice each apple into approximately 12 slices. In a medium mixing bowl, combine sugar, 1 T. cinnamon, and nutmeg. Add apple slices and toss to coat. Shake off any excess mixture and arrange the apple slices on the same baking sheet in a single layer. Bake slices in 400 degree oven until dark brown, caramelized, and tender, about 12–15 minutes. Remove from oven and let cool for 15 minutes.

To assemble the pies, place 4 baked pastry wedges on a serving platter or individual plates. Top each wedge with cooked apple slices. Dollop about 2 T.

whipped cream on top of each wedge and cover with remaining pastry wedges. Dust with a light sprinkling of cinnamon and serve immediately. A small scoop of vanilla ice cream can be served with each pie wedge.

Nutritional Information (per serving): Calories 417.6; Total Fat 21.3g; Cholesterol 0.0mg; Sodium 409.4mg; Total Carbohydrates 56.2g (Dietary Fiber 3.6g); Protein 2.8g

Ruth's Hot Fudge Sauce

*Serve over your favorite ice cream
for an easy after-dinner treat!*

Contributed by Ruth Holm—Littleton, Colorado

½ cup butter
1 cup chocolate chips
1–14 oz. can evaporated milk
2 cups sugar
1 t. vanilla

Recipe Yield

12 servings

Prep Time

20 minutes

Total Time

20 minutes

Directions

In a medium saucepan, melt butter and chocolate chips over low heat. Add evaporated milk and sugar. Stir well and bring to a boil over medium heat. Continue boiling for 5 minutes, stirring constantly. Remove fudge sauce from heat. Add vanilla, stir, and serve.

Nutritional Information (per serving): Calories 306.0; Total Fat 14.2g; Cholesterol 29.3mg; Sodium 88.6mg; Total Carbohydrates 45.3g (Dietary Fiber 2.1g); Protein 2.8g

Sour Cream Cookies

A soft cookie that melts in your mouth!

½ cup butter

1⅔ cups sugar

1 cup sour cream

3 eggs

3 cups flour

½ t. baking soda

1 t. vanilla

Recipe Yield

36 cookies

Prep Time

20 minutes

Total Time

45 minutes

Directions

Preheat oven to 350 degrees. Cream together butter and sugar on medium speed until fluffy. Add sour cream and mix for 30 seconds. Add eggs one at a time, mixing well. Combine flour and baking soda and add to butter mixture, mixing just until combined. Add vanilla and beat for 15 more seconds. Drop by tablespoon onto baking sheet and bake for approximately 10 minutes. Don't allow cookies to brown; they should spring back when gently pressed in the middle. Cool on wire rack.

Nutritional Information (per cookie): Calories 116.0; Total Fat 4.4g; Cholesterol 27.3mg; Sodium 44.5mg; Total Carbohydrates 17.5g (Dietary Fiber 0.3g); Protein 1.6g

Tiramisu

A delicious lighter version of a classic Italian favorite!

Espresso Drizzle

½ cup water
2 T. sugar
2 T. instant espresso granules
2 T. coffee-flavored liqueur (optional)

Cream Filling

1–8 oz. pkg. reduced fat cream cheese, softened
1–3.5 oz. carton mascarpone cheese
⅓ cup sugar
¼ cup brown sugar
2 t. coffee flavored liqueur, optional
24 cakelike ladyfingers
1½ t. unsweetened cocoa powder
½ oz. bittersweet or semisweet chocolate, grated

Recipe Yield	**Prep Time**	**Total time**
8 servings	30 minutes	3 hours 30 minutes

Directions

For espresso drizzle: combine the first 3 ingredients in a small saucepan over medium high heat; bring to a boil. Cook 1 minute more, stirring occasionally. Remove from heat and stir in 2 T. coffee-flavored liqueur, if using. Cool completely.

For cream filling: combine cream cheese and mascarpone cheese. Beat with an electric mixer until smooth. Add sugar, brown sugar, and remaining 2 t. coffee liqueur (if using), beating until well blended.

Split ladyfingers in half lengthwise. In the bottom of an 8 x 8 baking dish, arrange 24 ladyfinger halves, cut sides up. Drizzle half of the espresso sauce over the ladyfinger halves. Spread with half of the cheese filling. Repeat with remaining ladyfinger halves, espresso drizzle, and cream filling. Combine cocoa powder and grated chocolate; sprinkle evenly over top of filling. Cover with plastic wrap and then foil. Refrigerate for 3–5 hours, or freeze if you prefer more of an ice cream texture. Cut into squares and serve, dusting with additional cocoa powder or chocolate shavings if desired.

Nutritional Information (per serving): Calories 360.0; Total Fat 10.0g; Cholesterol 55.0mg; Sodium 317.0mg; Total Carbohydrates 38.4g (Dietary Fiber 0.5g); Protein 0.8g

White Chocolate Pudding with Strawberries

This pudding has a hint of lemon . . . very refreshing!

Contributed by Cassie Martinez—Lakewood, Colorado

2 large egg yolks
½ cup sugar
3 T. cornstarch
1¼ cups 2 percent milk
1½ cups heavy cream
4 oz. white chocolate, chopped
⅛ t. salt
¼ t. lemon oil
8 large strawberries

Recipe Yield

8 servings

Prep Time

25 minutes

Total Time

1 hour, 25 minutes

Directions

Whisk egg yolks, sugar, and cornstarch in a large bowl. Combine milk, heavy cream, white chocolate, and salt in a saucepan over medium heat and stir until the chocolate melts. Cool slightly (1 minute). Gradually pour the chocolate mixture into the egg mixture, whisking constantly. Pour back into saucepan and cook on low heat until thickened, 12–15 minutes. Remove from heat and stir in lemon oil. Divide pudding between 8 dessert cups. Cover with plastic wrap and refrigerate until set, about 1 hour.

When ready to serve, slice each strawberry nearly all the way through, beginning at the tip. Fan out each strawberry and place one on top of each pudding cup.

Nutritional Information (per serving): Calories 220.2; Total Fat 12.6g; Cholesterol 86.4mg; Sodium 73.6mg; Total Carbohydrates 24.2g (Dietary Fiber 0.0g); Protein 3.4g

Eliminating the Guesswork

Helpful Measurements, Equivalents, Weights, and Servings

Food Yields (these equivalents are only estimates to aid you when purchasing ingredients)

Food Item	Food Amount (Raw or Prepared)
Apple (1 medium)	1 cup chopped
Avocado (1 medium)	1 cup mashed or diced
Beans	
Dried (1 lb., 2 ½ cups)	6–7 cups cooked
Green/yellow, fresh (1 lb.)	2 cups cut
Breadcrumbs	
Dry (1 slice bread)	⅓ cup
Soft (1 slice bread)	¾ cup
Butter	
1 lb. (4 sticks)	2 cups
1 stick	½ cup or 8 T.
Carrots (2 medium)	1 cup diced or sliced
Celery (2 stalks)	1 cup diced or sliced
Cheese	
Cottage cheese (1 lb.)	2 cups
Cream cheese (8 oz.)	1 cup
Hard cheese (1 lb.)	4 cups grated
Soft cheese (1 lb.)	5 cups grated
Chicken breast, boneless	1 ½ cups cooked and diced
Chocolate (1 oz.)	1 square or 4 T.
Cilantro (1–4 oz. bunch)	2 ½ cups chopped
Garlic (1 medium clove)	½ t. chopped or pressed
Green or red bell pepper (1 medium)	¾ cup diced
Green onions, (2–3 stalks)	½–¾ cup
Lemon (1 medium)	2–3 T. juice; 2–3 t. grated zest
Lime (1 medium)	1 ½–2 T. juice

Food Item	Food Amount (Raw or Prepared)
Milk	
Evaporated (5.33 oz. can)	⅔ cup
Evaporated (14.5 oz. can)	1⅔ cups
Sweetened condensed (14 oz. can)	1⅓ cups
Whipping or heavy cream (1 cup)	2 cups whipped
Mushrooms (3–4 oz.)	1 cup sliced
Nuts	
Almonds (8 oz.)	1 cup sliced or chopped
Cashews (6 oz.)	1 cup
Pecans (8 oz.)	2 cups whole; 1¾ cups chopped
Walnuts (6 oz.)	1 cup
Onion	
1 medium	1 cup diced
1 lb.	3–3½ cups diced
Orange (1 medium)	½ cup juice; 1½–2 T. zest
Parsley (1–4 oz. bunch)	3½ cups chopped
Pasta	
macaroni (8 oz., 2 cups uncooked)	4 cups cooked
egg noodles (8 oz., 3 cups uncooked)	6 cups cooked
spaghetti (1 lb. uncooked)	7 cups cooked
Potatoes	
1 medium	½ cup diced; ¾ cup mashed
1 lb. (4 medium)	3½–4 cups diced; 2 cups mashed
Raisins (5 oz.)	1 cup
Rice	
1 cup, raw	3–3½ cups cooked
1 lb.	2½ cups uncooked
Spinach (10 oz., fresh)	12 cups loose packed; 1 cup cooked
Strawberries (1 pint)	2 cups sliced
Sugar	
Brown sugar (1 lb.)	2¼ cups packed
Granulated (1 lb.)	2 cups
Powdered (1 lb.)	3¾ cups unsifted
Tomatoes	
1 medium	¾ cup diced; ½ cup puree
1 lb. (3–4 medium)	2½ cups cooked
14 oz. canned	1½ cups with juice; ¾ cup drained

Baking Dish/Pan Equivalents

1 qt. dish	4 cup baking dish	9 inch pie plate	8 x 1 ½ inch round cake pan	7⅜ x 3⅝ x 2¼ inch loaf pan
1 ½ qt. dish	6 cup baking dish	10 inch pie plate	8 or 9 x 1 ½ inch round cake pan	8 ½ x 3⅝ x 2⅝ inch loaf pan
2 qt. dish	8 cup baking dish	8 x 8 x 2 inch square pan	11 x 7 x 1 ½ inch baking pan	9 x 5 x 3 inch loaf pan
2 ½ qt. dish	10 cup baking dish	9 x 9 x 2 inch square pan	11 ¾ x 7 ½ x 1 ¾ inch baking pan	9 x 5 x 3 inch loaf pan
3 qt. dish	12 cup baking dish	13 x 9 x 2 inch oblong pan		

Measurement Equivalents

Ounces	Tablespoon	Teaspoon	Cups
-	1	3	-
1	2	6	-
2	4	12	¼
-	5⅓	-	⅓
3	6	18	-
4	8	24	½
5	10	30	-
-	10⅔	-	⅔
6	12	36	¾
7	14	42	-
8	16	48	1

2 cups	1 pint
4 cups	1 quart
4 quarts	1 gallon
16 oz.	1 pound
32 oz.	1 quart

Metric Conversion Guide

VOLUME

U.S. Units	Metric
½ teaspoon	2 ml
1 teaspoon	5 ml
1 tablespoon	20 ml
¼ cup	60 ml
⅓ cup	80 ml
½ cup	125 ml
⅔ cup	170 ml
¾ cup	190 ml
1 cup	250 ml
1 quart	1 liter

TEMPERATURE

Fahrenheit	Celsius
250°	120°
275°	140°
300°	150°
325°	160°
350°	180°
375°	190°
400°	200°
425°	220°
450°	230°
475°	240°
500°	260°

LENGTH

Inches	Centimeters
1	2.5
2	5.0
3	7.5
4	10.0
5	12.5
6	15.0
7	17.5
8	20.5
9	23.0
10	25.5
11	28.0
12	30.5
13	33.0
14	35.5
15	38.0

WEIGHT

U.S. Units	Metric
1 ounce	30 grams
2 ounces	60 grams
3 ounces	90 grams
4 ounces (¼ pound)	125 grams
8 ounces (½ pound)	225 grams
16 ounces (1 pound)	500 grams

Note: The recipes in this cookbook have not been developed or tested using metric measures. When converting recipes to metric, some variations in quality may be noted.

Recipe Index

Susie Martinez is a professional counselor with a private counseling practice in Lakewood, Colorado. She has been married to her husband, Joe (whom she adores), for twenty-five years and has two children. Susie loves shopping and watching movies with her daughter, Cassie. She also loves talking with her son, Chris, during late-night hours. In her free time, Susie enjoys going to movies, taking long walks, and baking extravagant desserts. Susie also struggles with a particular weakness for island excursions and white sandy beaches.

Vanda Howell is a busy wife and mom who works part-time as a kitchen design consultant. She is absolutely in love with (aka addicted to) dark chocolate covered anything, espresso lattes, and going to chick-flick/action movies. In her free time she enjoys gardening, gourmet cooking, trying new restaurants, and wakeboarding with her husband and her teenage son, Elliott. Vanda is a Denver native, and has been married to her husband, Mike, for twenty-nine years.

Bonnie Garcia keeps busy with her husband, three teenage sons, and golden retriever, Gracie. She is a pediatric nurse and loves working with newborns and their parents in a pediatric practice in the Denver area. Bonnie is active in her local church, where her husband, Steve, is the senior pastor. In Bonnie's free time, she loves reading, downhill skiing, and jeeping with her family in the mountains of Colorado!

"I'm hungry. What's for dinner?"

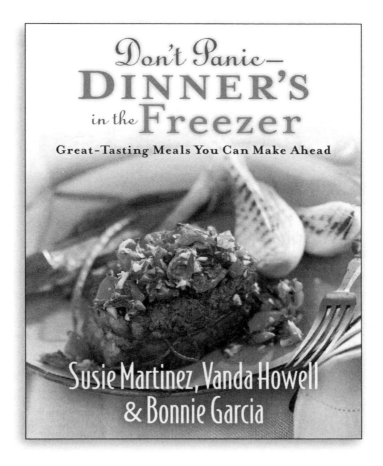

Harried, hurried, and hungry? Three experienced cooks share a simple and economical alternative to take-out and prepackaged foods. *Don't Panic—Dinner's in the Freezer* features dozens of quick and easy home-tested recipes.

R Revell
a division of Baker Publishing Group
www.RevellBooks.com

A Second Helping of Easy, Tasty Make–Ahead Recipes

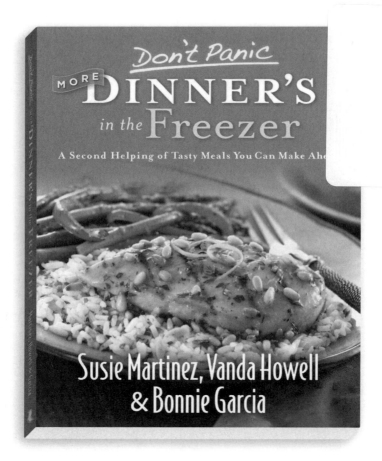

Three experienced cooks share more simple and economical alternatives to take-out and prepackaged foods. You will love these quick and healthful home-tested recipes.

Revell

a division of Baker Publishing Group
www.RevellBooks.com

Available wherever books are sold.